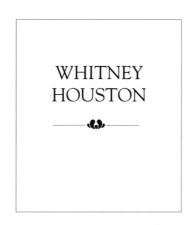

WHITNEY
HOUSTON

WHITNEY HOUSTON

Ted Cox

CHELSEA HOUSE PUBLISHERS
Philadelphia

Chelsea House Publishers

Editor-in-Chief	Stephen Reginald
Managing Editor	James D. Gallagher
Production Manager	Pamela Loos
Art Director	Sara Davis
Picture Editor	Judy Hasday
Senior Production Editor	Lisa Chippendale

Staff for WHITNEY HOUSTON

Senior Editor	Therese De Angelis
Associate Editor	Kristine Brennan
Associate Art Director	Takeshi Takahashi
Designer	Brian Wible
Picture Researcher	Patricia Burns
Cover Illustrator	Earl Parker

The Chelsea House World Wide Web site address is http://www.chelseahouse.com

3 5 7 9 8 6 4 2

Library of Congress Cataloging-in-Publication Data

Cox, Ted.
Whitney Houston / by Ted Cox.
104 pp.   cm. —(Black Americans of achievement)
Includes bibliographical references, discography, and index.
ISBN 0-7910-4455-6 (hardcover). — ISBN 0-7910-4456-4 (pbk.)
1. Houston, Whitney—Juvenile literature. 2. Singers—United
States—Biography—Juvenile literature. I. Series.
ML3930.H7C69 1997b
782.42164'092—dc21
[B]
                                        97-38158
                                           CIP
                                        AC MN

Frontis: Whitney Houston performing at the 1993 Billboard Music Awards ceremony, where she won 11 awards

CONTENTS

BLACK AMERICANS OF ACHIEVEMENT

HENRY AARON
baseball great

KAREEM ABDUL-JABBAR
basketball great

MUHAMMAD ALI
heavyweight champion

RICHARD ALLEN
religious leader and social activist

MAYA ANGELOU
author

LOUIS ARMSTRONG
musician

ARTHUR ASHE
tennis great

JOSEPHINE BAKER
entertainer

JAMES BALDWIN
author

BENJAMIN BANNEKER
scientist and mathematician

AMIRI BARAKA
poet and playwright

COUNT BASIE
bandleader and composer

ROMARE BEARDEN
artist

JAMES BECKWOURTH
frontiersman

MARY MCLEOD BETHUNE
educator

GEORGE WASHINGTON
CARVER
botanist

CHARLES CHESNUTT
author

BILL COSBY
entertainer

JOHNNIE COCHRAN
lawyer

PAUL CUFFE
merchant and abolitionist

MILES DAVIS
musician

FATHER DIVINE
religious leader

FREDERICK DOUGLASS
abolitionist editor

CHARLES DREW
physician

W. E. B. DU BOIS
scholar and activist

PAUL LAURENCE DUNBAR
poet

DUKE ELLINGTON
bandleader and composer

RALPH ELLISON
author

JULIUS ERVING
basketball great

LOUIS FARRAKHAN
political activist

ELLA FITZGERALD
singer

MARCUS GARVEY
black nationalist leader

JOSH GIBSON
baseball great

WHOOPI GOLDBERG
entertainer

CUBA GOODING JR.
actor

ALEX HALEY
author

PRINCE HALL
social reformer

JIMI HENDRIX
musician

MATTHEW HENSON
explorer

BILLIE HOLIDAY
singer

LENA HORNE
entertainer

WHITNEY HOUSTON
singer and actress

LANGSTON HUGHES
poet

ZORA NEALE HURSTON
author

JESSE JACKSON
civil-rights leader and politician

JANET JACKSON
musician

MICHAEL JACKSON
entertainer

SAMUEL L. JACKSON
actor

T. D. JAKES
religious leader

JACK JOHNSON
heavyweight champion

MAGIC JOHNSON
basketball great

SCOTT JOPLIN
composer

BARBARA JORDAN
politician

MICHAEL JORDAN
basketball great

CORETTA SCOTT KING
civil-rights leader

MARTIN LUTHER KING, JR.
civil-rights leader

LEWIS LATIMER
scientist

SPIKE LEE
filmmaker

CARL LEWIS
champion athlete

JOE LOUIS
heavyweight champion

RONALD MCNAIR
astronaut

MALCOLM X
militant black leader

BOB MARLEY
musician

THURGOOD MARSHALL
Supreme Court justice

TONI MORRISON
author

ELIJAH MUHAMMAD
religious leader

EDDIE MURPHY
entertainer

JESSE OWENS
champion athlete

SATCHEL PAIGE
baseball great

CHARLIE PARKER
musician

ROSA PARKS
civil-rights leader

COLIN POWELL
military leader

PAUL ROBESON
singer and actor

JACKIE ROBINSON
baseball great

CHRIS ROCK
comedian/actor

DIANA ROSS
entertainer

WILL SMITH
actor

CLARENCE THOMAS
Supreme Court justice

SOJOURNER TRUTH
antislavery activist

HARRIET TUBMAN
antislavery activist

NAT TURNER
slave revolt leader

DENMARK VESEY
slave revolt leader

ALICE WALKER
author

MADAM C. J. WALKER
entrepreneur

BOOKER T. WASHINGTON
educator

DENZEL WASHINGTON
actor

OPRAH WINFREY
entertainer

J. C. WATTS
politician

TIGER WOODS
golf star

RICHARD WRIGHT
author

ON
ACHIEVEMENT

❦

Coretta Scott King

Bᴇғᴏʀᴇ ʏᴏᴜ ʙᴇɢɪɴ this book, I hope you will ask yourself what the word *excellence* means to you. I think it's a question we should all ask, and keep asking as we grow older and change. Because the truest answer to it should never change. When you think of excellence, perhaps you think of success at work; or of becoming wealthy; or meeting the right person, getting married, and having a good family life.

Those goals are worth striving for, but there is a better way to look at excellence. As Martin Luther King Jr. said in one of his last sermons, "I want you to be first in love. I want you to be first in moral excellence. I want you to be first in generosity. If you want to be important, wonderful. If you want to be great, wonderful. But recognize that he who is greatest among you shall be your servant."

My husband knew that the true meaning of achievement is service. When I met him, in 1952, he was already ordained as a Baptist minister and was working toward a doctoral degree at Boston University. I was studying at the New England Conservatory and dreamed of accomplishments in music. We married a year later, and after I graduated the following year we moved to Montgomery, Alabama. We didn't know it then, but our notions of achievement were about to undergo a dramatic change.

You may have read or heard about what happened next. What began with the boycott of a local bus line grew into a national crusade, and by the time he was assassinated in 1968 my husband had fashioned a black movement powerful enough to shatter forever the practice of racial segregation. What you may not have read about is where he learned to resist injustice without compromising his religious beliefs.

He adopted a strategy of nonviolence from a man of a different race, who lived in a different country and even practiced a different religion. The man was Mahatma Gandhi, the great leader of India, who devoted his life to serving humanity in the spirit of love and nonviolence. It was in these principles that Martin discovered his method for social reform. More than anything else, those two principles were the key to his achievements.

These books are about African Americans who served society through the excellence of their achievements. They form part of the rich history of black men and women in America—a history of stunning accomplishments in every field of human endeavor, from literature and art to science, industry, education, diplomacy, athletics, jurisprudence, even polar exploration.

Not all of the people in this history had the same ideals, but I think you will find that all of them had something in common. Like Martin Luther King Jr., they all decided to become "drum majors" and serve humanity. In that principle—whether it was expressed in books, inventions, or song—they found a goal and a guide outside themselves that showed them a way to serve others instead of living only for themselves.

Reading the stories of these courageous men and women not only helps us discover the principles that we will use to guide our own lives; it also teaches us about our black heritage and about America itself. It is crucial for us to know the heroes and heroines of our history and to realize that the price we paid in our struggle for equality in America was dear. But we must also understand that we have gotten as far as we have partly because America's democratic system and ideals made it possible.

We are still struggling with racism and prejudice. But the great men and women in this series are a tribute to the spirit of the country in which they have flourished. And that makes their stories special and worth knowing.

1
HOW WILL I KNOW?

Whitney Houston was already a star when she arrived at the Grammy Awards ceremony on February 25, 1986. Her first album, *Whitney Houston*, had created a worldwide sensation in the music industry. Yet suddenly it seemed clear to everyone that she was poised on the brink of something else—recognition as a great artist. It had caught her completely by surprise. Her career and her entire life had been moving so fast that she hadn't even thought about the Grammy Awards. Yet here she was, at 22 years old, nominated for three awards at the Grammys, the most prestigious annual event in the music industry. As if this weren't an amazing enough prospect, her cousin, Dionne Warwick, was onstage to present the award for Best Pop Vocal Performance by a Female.

Whitney was competing in this category against some of the biggest names in music. Madonna, nominated for "Crazy for You," was a young, up-and coming star like her, but there were also established talents like Linda Ronstadt, Pat Benatar, and soul singer Tina Turner. Whitney had already lost in the Best R&B (rhythm-and-blues) Solo Performance category, which, if anything, had been even more competitive. Teena Marie had been nominated in that category along with Whitney, Patti LaBelle, Aretha Franklin, and Chaka Khan. As a teenager, Whitney had once sung backup for Chaka along with

Twenty-two-year-old Whitney Houston proudly displays her 1986 Grammy Award for Best Pop Vocal Performance by a Female.

her mother, Cissy Houston, a great soul singer in her own right. But the winner had been Aretha Franklin, who had enjoyed a big comeback in 1985 with the rollicking single "Freeway of Love." Aretha was Whitney's godmother, known to her as "Auntie Ree." Franklin had also used Whitney's mother Cissy as a background singer, starting in the 1960s. For Whitney, the experience of being in the same league as these luminaries was new, and yet so many of them were familiar to her.

She tried to remain calm about it all. "If I win, I win," she said. "It's an honor, of course, but I feel the same as I did before," she reminded herself.

Only a year before, when *Whitney Houston* was released, she had been a virtual unknown. People in the music industry knew about her, though. She was the protégé of Clive Davis, head of Arista Records, a man known for spotting and developing talent. He had signed Whitney to an extended contract and had spent $250,000 recording her debut album. But not even industry insiders had expected the results to be so stunning. Working with four producers, she had shown her mastery of a variety of styles. Her repertoire included the soulful "You Give Good Love" and "All at Once," the ballads "Saving All My Love for You" and "Greatest Love of All," and then the dance hit "How Will I Know," which had just climbed to the top of the singles charts. The album had already sold 3 million copies and was on its way to eventually topping the 20-million mark worldwide—making it the best-selling solo debut album in history.

Up until this point in her meteoric career, Whitney had managed to keep her composure as far as her public persona was concerned; but it was admittedly thrilling for her to travel the world and perform in front of adoring crowds. Away from the stage, however, she said her life had remained very much the same as it had always been. "It's just gotten busier and faster," she explained. She was determined to "keep

Whitney (left) hugs her cousin, Dionne Warwick, who presented her with the 1986 Grammy Award for her song "Saving All My Love for You."

[her] feet on the ground no matter how big things get." But now, as she was being recognized alongside the biggest names in music, the excitement was almost too much for Whitney.

Yet it wasn't quite enough for Clive Davis. When the Grammy nominations had been announced, he was angry that Whitney had been passed over in the Best New Artist category—because of a technicality. While Whitney had been preparing her debut album, she had recorded duets with Teddy Pendergrass and Jermaine Jackson. Both songs had been released as singles the year before, and they had done well. But their release made Whitney ineligible for consideration in the Best New Artist of 1985 category. Davis had gone so far as to write a letter of protest in the editorial section of the industry magazine *Billboard*.

"How is it," he wrote, "that a recording artist can be voted favorite new female artist by the readers of *Rolling Stone*, named newcomer of the year in music by [the TV show] *Entertainment Tonight*, top new artist by *Billboard*, sell nearly 4 million copies worldwide of her very first album, and not be considered a candidate for best new artist by the National Academy of Recording Arts and Sciences?"

Yet Whitney took it in stride. It was enough for her that her peers had nominated her in the R&B category, as well as for Best Album and Best Pop Vocal Performance by a Female Artist. She tried to tell herself that it was honor enough to be nominated without even taking home an award at this stage of her career. But her cousin Dionne was about to name the winner in the pop category.

Dionne smiled and then let out a scream of joy before reading Whitney's name as the winner for "Saving All My Love for You." Whitney accepted the award with thanks to "God, who makes it all possible for me," and also to her parents, Cissy and John Houston, "the two most important people in my life." She had sung with her mother in church, then later in recording studios and New York City clubs. When she finally struck out on her own, the public had loved her. And now her fellow artists were saying she was the best pop singer of the year. Where would it all end?

"I just want to grow up to be me," Whitney had said not long before the Grammy ceremony. "We're talking about longevity." The question was, who was the real Whitney Houston, and how could she emerge when the public hungered for more of the star—who shared her face and figure but sometimes seemed so different?

Whitney had grown up a shy and oftentimes lonely girl in New Jersey. She had a strong family background; she also had a pedigree rich in vocal talent from her mother and her singing family, which included Dionne Warwick. Her singing had constantly attracted attention from the time she was a young teenager. Cissy Houston had actually discouraged a career in music at first, but in hindsight, it seemed as if the concerned mother was simply forestalling the inevitable.

At 22, Whitney was certainly a cheerful, attractive young woman, but she was hardly the ever-effervescent girl she was being portrayed as in the media, in magazine layouts, and in TV commercials. Where would her career take her, and how much control could she exert over it? It was just the beginning of a wild ride that would see her record a series of hit albums and move on to star in blockbuster Hollywood movies. All the while, she would deal with fans, reporters, and TV interviewers who forever wanted to know more about her—as long as the truth lived up to their preconceptions. She would experience some difficult stretches, both personally and professionally, punctuated by the joys of friendship, marriage, and motherhood. Whitney's early life practically groomed her for stardom, but she would also put her unique stamp on her music and on her career as she slowly, and sometimes painfully, came to terms with that stardom. In small increments, she would mature and reveal the real Whitney Houston to the public.

"Everybody thinks that because you have this so-called fame and fortune, you have the so-called good life," she said much later on, looking back. "It is a good life. God knows that when he blesses you, you are blessed. But sometimes you work for that life. You pay a price for that life, and all of a sudden it isn't 'the good life' so much."

Friends, family, fame, fortune—they all came together for Whitney on the night she won her first Grammy. But it would take years for her to learn how to keep those various elements of her life in perspective and in balance. Along the way, she would establish herself as the most powerful singer of her generation and one of the most sought-after actresses in feature films. But Whitney's struggle for selfhood would prove to be even more difficult than maintaining her career—and, in the end, far more satisfying.

2
TOMORROW

Whitney Houston was born on August 9, 1963, in East Orange, New Jersey, the third child and only daughter of John and Cissy Houston. She was named after the actress Whitney Blake, one of the costars of the hit sitcom *Hazel*. Cissy, impressed by Blake's elegance in an era when few black actresses portrayed classy, intelligent women, hoped that the name would bring her baby similar success. Cissy Houston was a successful background singer in soul music, and John had also been an aspiring singer before devoting himself to managing Cissy's career.

"The talent I have, I inherited from my mother and my family," Whitney would say later on. "They've certainly all helped me—that's no secret—and not just by being relatives, although that's an asset. It's the support and sacrifices of my family that have really counted. I'm very proud and honored to have that blood running through my veins."

In fact, Cissy had been pursuing a singing career since long before Whitney was born, and she kept at it right through her pregnancy, just as she had before Whitney's older brother Michael arrived. Cissy Houston recorded throughout the summer before Whitney's birth, commuting to music studios in New York City from the family's New Jersey home.

"Mommy said the producers were real jittery" about having a very pregnant singer at their record-

Whitney with her parents, John and Cissy Houston, in 1986.

ing sessions, Whitney later explained, "but she just told them to quit worrying and get on with it."

Cissy's drive—as well as her sheer talent—would later be passed on to Whitney. Cissy, whose given name was Emily Drinkard, was the youngest of eight children. She had first made a name for herself in the early 1960s with a gospel singing group called the Drinkard Sisters, which included her cousin, Lee Warrick Drinkard, and Lee's two daughters, Dee Dee and Marie Dionne Warrick. Marie Dionne would soon drop her first name, alter the spelling of her last name, and go on to a stellar career as Dionne Warwick, a smooth and stylish interpreter of hits for renowned songwriters Burt Bacharach and Hal David. Her hits include such signature songs of the 1970s as "I Say a Little Prayer." Dionne's rise to fame would prove to be an inspiration for Whitney.

"What I got from Dionne was the class and elegance and the radiance, how she commands an audience," Whitney would later acknowledge.

"With her looks and talent, she had all the credentials," Warwick would respond, calling Whitney "the little girl I never had." She continued, "Her success was something that was supposed to happen. And, like all of us in the family, Whitney was singing from the moment she came out."

As a child, however, Whitney's greatest inspiration was her mother. In 1965, Cissy formed a new group called Cissy's Girls, which was later renamed the Sweet Inspirations. The Sweet Inspirations backed up Aretha Franklin, Elvis Presley, and many other acts both on tour and in the studio. In fact, Aretha was Whitney's godmother, and around the age most little girls start kindergarten, Whitney began accompanying her mother to the studio.

"She was always there, in my face," said the woman Whitney called "Auntie Ree." "I loved her. She wanted to sing. I knew that even then. She was always watching closely, whispering to her mother.

She had great spirit. She sang in the corner, always humming to herself, trying to duplicate the sounds she was hearing. She'd say, 'I want to be a Sweet Inspiration too.' "

Simply watching Franklin at work was an education for Whitney. "Aretha has such a gut about what she's singing," Houston would later remark. "I said, 'I want to feel like that. I want to be able to make people feel like she's making them feel.'

"Being around people like Aretha Franklin and Gladys Knight, Dionne Warwick and Roberta Flack, all these greats, I was taught to listen and observe," Whitney remembered. "It had a great impact on me as a singer, as a performer, as a musician. Growing up around it, you just can't help it. I identified with it immediately. It was something that was so natural that when I started singing, it was almost like speaking.

"I just remember being in an atmosphere of total creativity," Whitney added. "It was lots of fun, but I wasn't spoiled in any way. I did get to experience a lot of things that maybe other kids didn't, like being around other entertainers. But I got to know them like they were my family, and contrary to what other people may think about being a show-business brat and all that, it wasn't like that at all."

Cissy made sure all the members of her family maintained a clear sense of perspective regarding celebrity, perhaps because she herself never became as big a star as she had expected. For years, she was one of the most sought-after background singers for albums recorded by world-famous acts, but for one reason or another, stardom had always eluded her. One group album, entitled *Sweet Inspiration*, did produce a top-20 single, but Cissy's star never rose after that. She knew how capricious the entertainment industry could be, so she made sure her children kept their feet firmly on the ground—even when hobnobbing with stars other kids only dreamed of meeting.

Whitney's earliest musical inspirations included her cousin, Dionne Warwick (left), and her mother, gospel singer Cissy Houston.

"Cissy was a great mother," remembered Pat Mikell, a New York City club owner and family friend. "She was tough. That's why Whitney's a class act."

"My family and I are very close, and growing up for me was a lot of fun," Whitney said. "I had a regular childhood, and I was a little girl when I was supposed to be, and when I had to be a teenager I enjoyed those years. My parents were exceptionally good at raising children. They gave my brothers and me guidance at a time when we didn't know what to do, and kept us at a pace so we could lead normal lives. My mother made sure we had a normal childhood."

Whitney grew up with two older brothers: Michael and half-brother Gary Garland, a child from Cissy's first marriage. Gary would later go on to become a basketball star at DePaul University in Chicago—yet another member of the family to distinguish himself. But they had fairly typical childhoods even though the family lived in the rough section of Newark, New Jersey, throughout Cissy and

John's struggles to jump-start her career.

"When the children were little, we had family meetings all the time, where everyone expressed their feelings," Cissy recalled. "If the children believed we had wronged them, they could say so, without fear of being punished or thought disobedient."

Despite her parents' very open manner, Whitney was shy with strangers and in public settings like school. But at home her father considered her a "talkative, independent" child. Her brother Gary later remembered her "dressed up in mother's gowns, down in the basement, singing her lungs out like she was in Madison Square Garden." Whitney herself declared, "Being that I was the only girl, you would think that I had it rough. I did. But I must admit I wouldn't have wanted it any other way."

When the race riots that struck Newark in 1967 threatened to make life rougher still, the family moved to the slightly more well-to-do area of East Orange. The move put more pressure on Cissy to build a successful career, which in turn placed more demands on her time and threatened to cut into her already-scarce family time. One of the ways she would try to bring music and family together was through church life and gospel music. "I grew up in a church family, and I started singing gospel when I was five," Whitney has said. "I was singing gospel before I could pronounce the words." She went on:

> Gospel music has always been the center of our lives. It taught me a lot about singing. It gave me emotion and spiritual things, and it helped me to know what I was singing about, because in gospel music, the words mean everything. Now whatever I sing, whether it's gospel or pop or R & B, I feel it. I think I got my emotion from gospel singing, from my mom instilling it in me at an early age. You can't make people feel anything you don't feel yourself.

"Music was all around our house," she remembered. "There was the gospel music, but my parents listened to everything else too—rhythm & blues, jazz, pop." Such eclectic early influences would later serve Whitney well, enabling her to master many singing styles.

Whitney sang her first solo, "Guide Me, Oh Thou Great Jehovah," at the age of 11 at the New Hope Baptist Church in Newark, where Cissy served as minister of music. "I stood there stiff as a board," Whitney remembered, "but I sang this song and the people went crazy.

"I was scared to death," she added. "I was aware of people staring at me. No one moved. They seemed almost in a trance. I just stared at the clock in the center of the church. When I finished, everyone clapped and started crying. From then on, I knew God had blessed me."

Her auspicious debut launched speculation that Whitney would follow her mother into a recording career. But Cissy, who knew how hard it was to make a living in music, wasn't keen on the idea. She encouraged Whitney to develop other talents.

"I wanted to be a teacher," Whitney said. "I love children, so I wanted to deal with children. Then I wanted to be a veterinarian. But by the age of 10 or 11, when I opened my mouth and said, 'Oh God, what's this?' I kind of knew teaching and being a veterinarian were going to have to wait. What's in your soul is in your soul."

At first, Cissy limited Whitney to performing with the New Hope Baptist Junior Choir. But that did not prevent the young singer from having a busy schedule. "Church was a family function," Whitney said. "Every Sunday that came I went to church. I was in church Sunday, Monday, Tuesday, skipped Wednesday because that was adult choir rehearsal. I was back Thursday, Friday, Saturday, and then again Sunday."

John and Cissy took an equally vigilant attitude toward Whitney's schoolwork. Even in East Orange, the public schools could sometimes prove to be a rough environment. "In grammar school, some of the girls had problems with me," Whitney recalled. "My face was too light. My hair was too long. It was the black-consciousness period, and I felt really bad. I finally faced the fact that it isn't a crime not having friends. Being alone means you have fewer problems. When I decided to be a singer, my mother warned me I'd be alone a lot. Basically we all are. Loneliness comes with life."

When Whitney's teen years arrived, her parents pulled her out of the public schools and sent her to Mount St. Dominic Academy in nearby Caldwell. "My mother took me and put me in an all-girls school and said, 'No, girl. You're going *this* way, and this is what we're going to do here,'" Whitney recalled. Cissy and John laid down the law: she'd have to finish school before embarking on any kind of music career. "So I took their advice and just waited," Whitney said. The wait was hard on her, though.

The Houstons had always had a close family life, and Whitney was known as a daddy's girl. John's pet name for her was Nippy. "My dad is the backbone of our family. Any problem that I've ever had, he's always been there for me," she said. "I have a great dad. My father stuck by my mother and was a good friend to her. If my mother had a recording session, he would stay home, dress me, and do my hair. He would put a beautiful dress on me with tube socks— like sweat socks. And my hair would look kind of crooked, but it was cute. He was a very affectionate and loving dad.

"He was Mom's support network while she was on tour," Whitney added. "He changed diapers, cooked, did my hair, and dressed me, all the while providing Mom with advice and answers."

But by the late 1970s the strains of being husband, father, and manager were beginning to show in John's relationship with Cissy. The couple split up in

1977, and Whitney was devastated. The divorce, however, would prove to have natural, if unintended, benefits for the family.

Her parents actually got along better after the breakup. "They'd laugh a lot," Whitney remembered, "and when times were hard they fought, which taught me a lot about love and sacrifice. For a while they stayed together for our sake. Finally they realized that the only way for them to stay friends was to split. It was strange not to have my father there, but he lived just 10 minutes away. Besides, even if you're not together physically, the love never dies."

"We love each other," Cissy would later explain. "Whatever happens, we'll always love each other."

Whitney also got a closer look at her mother's work. Cissy knew she'd have to spend more time with Whitney, so she started taking her more often to studio sessions and live performances. By this time, Cissy had largely given up singing background in favor of a solo career. She had never had a hit record as a solo artist, but by the late 1970s she was a well-known cabaret singer in New York City and began including Whitney in her shows. This marked the beginning of an apprenticeship for Whitney—from which she would eventually emerge as the star attraction.

"She's the master, I'm the student," Whitney would say of her mother with a laugh after becoming famous in her own right. "She has greater range, greater power than I ever did." In 1978, at the age of 15, Whitney was granted a solo by Cissy during a performance at New York's famed Town Hall.

"I was pretty nervous," Whitney said later, recalling the tumult of emotions she felt. "I was scared to death. It was fun. I just fell in love with my mom!"

From then on, Whitney would sing background and be given an occasional solo, such as "Tomorrow" from the Broadway hit *Annie* or "Greatest Love of All," a lesser-known ballad she would later make

Whitney's godmother, Aretha Franklin, is known to her as "Auntie Ree," but to music fans as "Lady Soul."

famous. People marveled at Whitney's untapped talent and her three-octave range. But Cissy was determined to protect Whitney from being pushed into a music career. She constantly admonished her daughter to keep her sense of perspective, dispensing such advice as "You want pride, not ego" and "To thine own self be true." If she caught Whitney hamming it up onstage, or thinking too much of herself offstage, Cissy would eliminate Whitney's solos for a performance or two. But she had her daughter's best interests at heart in doing so.

Cissy also took an acute interest in Whitney's

Although Whitney worked for some time as a professional model, she never gave up her dream of a successful music career.

personal life. "She didn't date young," Cissy said. "I didn't allow it. Period. But she did go through a rebellious teenage phase, mostly small stuff—staying out late, not washing the dishes. "She was lazy, stubborn, and opinionated. When she was 16 I told her she wasn't going to make it to 17 because I was going to kill her."

Cissy kept pounding advice into her daughter's memory: "Be aware! Observe! Learn to distinguish good friends, real friends, from those who are your friends for a reason, friends who have an agenda." Cissy knew a recording career would take an immense investment in time; school and a relatively normal childhood came first, she said. Nonetheless, other events would persistently push Whitney toward stardom.

Whitney and Cissy were walking down the street in New York City one day in 1978 when they were stopped by a man who claimed to work for a modeling agency. He wanted to recruit Whitney as a model. At first, they thought he was crazy; he turned out to be legitimate, however. He worked for Click Models, and when Whitney was introduced to the agency's owner, he signed her on the spot.

Photo shoots—unlike musical tours—could be arranged around a classroom schedule. Cissy had no objections to Whitney's new opportunity; in fact, her mother hoped it might distract her from music for awhile. Whitney's natural good looks soon earned her fashion spreads in *Glamour*, *Cosmopolitan*, and *Young Miss*, and she moved up to the more prestigious Wilhelmina Modeling Agency. But her success never diverted her from what she really wanted to do.

"The camera and I were great friends. I know the eye of the camera is on me—eye to eye. It loves me, and I love it," she said. "I like modeling, but singing was in my blood."

3
ALL AT ONCE

When Whitney Houston graduated from Mount St. Dominic Academy and began concentrating on music, she found that not only did her mother no longer stand in her way, but Cissy's experience in the music business actually offered Whitney a wealth of opportunities. Although Cissy had never been a big star in her own right, she had plenty of contacts and knew plenty of people who were eager to see and hear the young woman who combined a model's looks—she had filled out at five feet, eight inches tall and 115 pounds—with Cissy's voice. If Cissy thought Whitney was good enough to bring along to a recording session, that was recommendation enough for most people.

Cissy had provided background vocals on Chaka Khan's 1978 solo debut, *Chaka*, which included the hit single "I'm Every Woman." (Whitney would later incorporate that song into the soundtrack album for *Waiting to Exhale*.) When Chaka returned to the studio to record the followup, *Naughty*, in 1980, so did Cissy, and she brought Whitney with her. Whitney appeared on the songs "Clouds" and "Our Love's in Danger." She also earned backing credits on albums by the Neville Brothers and Lou Rawls.

The music business was beginning to buzz. No less than *Billboard* magazine, in a review of one of

Whitney belts out a song during a benefit concert in Boston.

Cissy's New York shows, said, "Whitney has the pedigree and the style to be a major vocalist."

In 1981, Cissy oversaw Whitney's choice of an agent, Eugene Harvey. And offers started rolling in. They weren't yet coming from the popular acts in the music industry, but they were prestigious. The avant-garde New York jazz-funk band Material chose Whitney to sing lead vocals on "Memories," a song on its critically acclaimed 1982 album *One Down*. The Village Voice's Robert Christgau, known as "the dean of American rock critics," called it "one of the most gorgeous ballads you've ever heard."

Today, "Memories" sounds like Whitney taking her first steps toward greatness. What's remarkable about her performance is her restraint at an age when most young singers are eager to show off their pipes. Even when Whitney threatens to cut loose, as she does toward the end, she keeps things under control. She leaves it to saxophonist Oliver Lake, on loan from the renowned jazz group the World Saxophone Quartet, to convey the song's emotion, and in the process she gives a performance far beyond her years.

At about the same time, Paul Shaffer, who would later go on to stardom as the bandleader for *Late Night with David Letterman*, enjoyed a novelty hit with a group called the Weather Girls. When he and Paul Jabara, who had cowritten the song called "It's Raining Men," rushed to record an album to support the single, Whitney was in the right place at the right time. The album, *Paul Jabara and Friends, Featuring the Weather Girls, Leata Galloway, and Whitney Houston*, didn't set any sales records, but it did provide Whitney with her first title credit.

Hers was not a direct path to stardom. Another of Whitney's lesser-known early gigs was singing background vocals on advertisements for Bounce fabric softeners. But she was still just a teenager, and for Whitney Houston, things were about to start moving very fast indeed. Her new agent arranged a commercial for Canada Dry soft drinks, as well as appearances on the TV situation comedies *Silver Spoons* and *Gimme a Break.*

During this period, Whitney continued to perform in New York cabarets with her mother. In 1982, she came to the notice of *Village Voice* critic Don Shewey. Reviewing Cissy's show, he wound up gushing over 18-year-old Whitney instead. "She sang in long, unfussy lines," Shewey wrote,

> building slowly and holding off forever a gorgeous vibrato she deployed very sparingly and only after throwing in a few blocky gospel phrases almost as a surprise. She didn't wring the tunes dry or scrape them clean or anything like that—no violence, no overkill. The widest open note was controlled and clear as the hum she produced by holding the word 'time' with her lips closed; every note there was wanted. These are the best habits for a young singer to have.

Elektra Records, Material's label, was ready to sign Whitney, and Cissy was agreeable. But then one night a man named Gerry Griffith caught Cissy's show in New York, with Whitney again in fine voice. Griffith was a well-known talent scout for Arista Records impresario Clive Davis. He brought back a glowing report on Whitney and arranged an audition. Davis had built Columbia Records into a powerhouse before going off to form his own label, Arista. He had long been a fan of Dionne Warwick, another Arista artist. When he heard Whitney sing, he was impressed by her voice but did not immediately share in Griffith's unadulterated enthusiasm. But Griffith allegedly convinced him of Whitney's superstar potential; and when he realized that Whitney was in demand elsewhere, Davis reconsidered. He promised to take a strong hand in guiding Whitney's career, and Cissy liked that.

Rhythm-and-blues singer Chaka Khan, shown here at the 1985 Grammy Awards. One of Whitney Houston's earliest recording opportunities was as a background vocalist for Chaka Khan's 1980 album Naughty.

"I did showcases and invited record-company people," Whitney remembered.

People were interested in me from the time I was 15—it was kind of like they were waiting for me to grow up. Everybody put their bids in. So I sat down with my managers and my parents, and I remember this long, drawn-out meeting. "What are you gonna do? Who are you going to go with?" I remember stopping the meeting and saying, "I've got to take a break." I went into another room and sat in a chair, and my mother came in after me and said, "You know, this is very difficult, but I'm going to tell you the truth. You should go where you are going to get the best out of it." Meaning, let's say a company offers you a contract and they're saying, "Whitney, you can choose the songs. You can produce the songs. You can do whatever you want to do." As opposed to Arista, with Clive Davis saying, "We'll give you this amount of money, and we'll sit down, and as far as the songs you want to do, I will help you. I will say, 'Whitney, this song has potential. This song doesn't.'" So my mother was saying to me, "You're 18 years old. You need guidance." Clive was the person who guided me.

Whitney signed with Arista Records.

Clive Davis knew how to build interest in a young act, especially in someone as talented as Whitney. When Merv Griffin planned to do a salute to Davis on his nationally syndicated talk show, Davis arranged to showcase Whitney as one of his new discoveries. "You either got it or you don't," he said in introducing her. "She's got it." Whitney did a terrific rendition of "Home." The buzz began to build.

Soul singer Teddy Pendergrass was making a comeback after suffering a tragic auto accident that had cost him the use of his legs. His hit single "You're My Choice Tonight (Choose Me)" had featured Cissy on background vocals. When he decided to do a full-fledged duet, he asked Whitney to join him. Davis agreed to let Whitney record for Pendergrass and Elektra if the song could also be used on Whitney's debut album. Pendergrass agreed, and "Hold Me" got Whitney on the charts with a hit single in 1984.

Davis next paired Whitney with Jermaine Jackson, who had recently joined the Arista stable as an artist and producer. Their duet, "Take Good Care of My Heart," also hit the charts. Whitney was then featured at Jackson's New York City record-release party, and after that at another high-profile affair celebrating Arista's 10th anniversary. Davis also arranged for Jackson and Houston to sing the duet "Nobody Loves Me Like You Do" on the popular TV soap opera *As the World Turns.*

By now, the whole industry was wondering when Whitney would have her own album out. But Davis wasn't rushing things. "She has such range, from theatrical to gospel to soul," he said. He wanted Whitney's debut to show off all her talents, from ballads to up-tempo R&B. He brought in four producers: in addition to Jackson, there was Michael Masser, who had worked with Pendergrass; Kashif, who contributed the ballad "You Give Good Love"; and Narada Michael Walden, who gave Whitney the danceable single "How Will I Know" at the same time he was recording Aretha Franklin's comeback single, "Who's Zoomin' Who?" and her hit song "Freeway of Love."

But it wasn't just record-industry bigwigs and other media muckety-mucks who were taking notice. Whitney was also impressing her fellow musicians. "She's very poised," said Bashiri Johnson, a percussionist on the "You Give Good Love" recording sessions, "and she's kind of like a cat—a panther. A panther will only strike when it needs to, but it has the capacity to be real powerful. That's the way she is. She's so powerful and awesome, and it's all under harness. She has control of it."

Kenneth Reynolds, head of R&B product management for Arista, said he was struck by Houston's presence at the filming of her first video, "You Give Good Love." "She came there like a real polished professional," he said, "which is a quality that I noticed in everything that she did. She may have been new to the business, but she conducted herself like someone who had really been around from day one. . . . I don't think that I have met anyone initially who was so young in their career, and yet so sure about themselves. . . . And so sure of what they wanted."

In all, Whitney's debut album, *Whitney Houston*, cost $250,000 to produce. Davis was taking no chances; he was carefully constructing her image. The fruits of no fewer than 10 separate album-cover photo sessions were eventually culled down to the elegant portrait that made the front cover—an African-American princess in fashionable pastels—and the sizzling bathing suit shot on the back. Arista

then sent out beach towels bearing that bathing suit shot to members of the media to further generate interest. That publicity shot would later lead to charges that Whitney was little more than a puppet manipulated by Davis—charges that Whitney would battle for years despite her own obvious musical talent.

Yet there was no doubting the sound behind the image, and there is still no doubting it today. Many promising young music acts get a big initial push from record companies, but Whitney consistently delivers the goods. The debut album begins with "You Give Good Love," and Whitney displays admirable restraint in her singing style. There is a moment when her voice almost cracks, but then she kicks it into a higher pitch that is totally under control. Kashif, who also produced the opener, then adds the next number, "Thinking About You." It's a

Clive Davis (left) signed Whitney to Arista Records, then spent two years promoting her and preparing her debut album. The time and effort paid off— the album sold 20 million copies, and four singles went to Number 1 on the Billboard charts.

formulaic, somewhat stiff mid-1980s pop-funk song in the Madonna mold, but worse than the writing is the production, especially the way Kashif echoes Whitney's vocals and blurs the fine points of her singing. From there, the album immediately recovers with the Jermaine Jackson-produced "Someone for Me." It has a funky bass line, and Whitney lets it settle into a groove before letting her voice dominate the song. The lyrics, about an innocent young girl of 17 yearning for release, suit Whitney's restrained singing style perfectly.

"Saving All My Love for You," however, is the place on that first album where Whitney proves she belongs in the same league as the great singers. The song—produced by Michael Masser, who cowrote it with Gerry Goffin—is a state-of-the-art mid-1980s ballad. It features Los Angeles studio great Tom Scott on saxophone. Despite her youth, Whitney is up to their level and, in fact, throws in some great touches of her own, most obviously in the way she puts a little grit, time and again, into the middle of a line before ending it with a soaring high note.

Jermaine Jackson and Teddy Pendergrass were both recruited to sing duets in what appeared to have been a favor to Whitney and Clive Davis, but the surprising thing about her debut album is that those duets have failed to stand the test of time the way her solo material has. Jackson's "Nobody Loves Me Like You Do" brings the first album side to a close. What's noticeable about Jackson's performance is the way he settles into playing second fiddle to Whitney's lovely trills, much as he had been a supporting singer to his brother Michael in their Jackson 5 days. Narada Michael Walden's rollicking "How Will I Know" jump-starts the album's second half. As the music settles into a groove, Whitney has the courage and the confidence to push the tempo, stressing the impatience of the singer to find out if she has found true love. As Whitney sings the chorus, "How will I know?" Cissy makes her lone appearance on the album to chime in with some advice in the background: "Trust your feelings." Walden's slack bridge on the album cut was later punched up by Madonna producer Jellybean Benitez for the dance-mix single release.

"All at Once" is another great Whitney ballad performance on par with "Saving All My Love for You." The song, written by producer Masser and smooth soul singer Jeffrey Osborne, is a tune about lost love, opening with a scene-setting electric piano instrumental. The hallmark of her style in this number is that way she uses her amazing vocal technique to channel the grief of the lyrics. Many critics would later find fault with Whitney on that count, suggesting that she was nothing but an emotionless, though technically brilliant, automaton. But the key to Whitney's greatness is the way she belies her grief by throwing herself into technique, much as a grief-stricken woman in real life might throw herself into her work. The lyrics suggest this when she sings, "And it hurts me more than you know/So much more than it shows."

After that impressive performance, the album breaks the mood again with the shimmering pop of Jackson's "Take Good Care of My Heart." Then comes Whitney's signature song, "The Greatest Love of All," in which she conveys pride and self-worth with a performance that rises to the level of producer Masser's powerful musical crescendo. Finally, the album closes with "Hold Me," Whitney's duet with Pendergrass, and she demonstrates a captivating knack for mimicking Pendergrass's smoky delivery before hitting her own vocal stride. "Hold Me" is not some tenderhearted ballad about a woman pleading for comfort; it is instead a song about two grown-up and experienced lovers meeting on equal footing.

The media were wowed by the new star with the

To build interest in Whitney's career, Clive Davis arranged for the young singer to perform on the television soap opera As the World Turns *with Jermaine Jackson. Whitney also sang a duet with Jermaine on the former Jackson 5 member's album.*

passionate voice and the fresh elegance of youth. "It will take an act of Congress to keep this woman from becoming a megastar," wrote *People* magazine. "Whitney Houston is a little frightening," said *Newsweek.* "No one person should have this much star quality. It doesn't seem fair."

If that sort of praise seemed excessive, it was tame next to the public's response to the album. "It was like a bomb went off," recalled one Hollywood record store manager. "We had barely unpacked the albums before a near riot broke out. I'd never seen so many kids in my life! The store was swarming with them, all clamoring for the Whitney Houston album. We were completely sold out in three days."

Whitney Houston would eventually sell 13 million copies in America and 20 million worldwide, making it the biggest debut album in music history at that time. Whitney was on her way.

And welcoming Whitney to stardom was her cousin Dionne Warwick. "It's nice to know the world's recognizing Whitney for the enormous talent that she is," she said. "Whitney's got the genes to be a star for a long time."

4

WHITNEY

❦

Whitney Houston was released in February 1985. Whitney won her first Grammy in February 1986. Over the course of those 12 months, she underwent many changes. First came a two-and-a-half-week concert tour in Europe, which was really the first time she had been out on her own, let alone traveled the world.

"I cried every day," she said when she got home. "You've got to remember that I'm still relatively young. I'm still a baby in a lot of senses."

She came home only to hit the road again in May, playing small clubs like the Roxy in Los Angeles and the Park West in Chicago. That summer, she was the opening act on Jeffrey Osborne's concert tour. But the opening act was soon more popular than the headliner. That fall, she played a pair of sold-out solo shows at New York City's Carnegie Hall. Whitney would never again open for anyone else; from now on, she was the headliner.

New York Times music critic John Pareles called her "an extraordinary singer whose flexible, rangy pop-gospel voice has a core of steel," dubbing her "the heir apparent to the female soul tradition of Aretha Franklin, Gladys Knight, and her first cousin Dionne Warwick." *Newsweek* magazine chimed in: "The years she spent in a Newark, N.J., Baptist choir, which her mother directs, are evident

Whitney sings one of her hits in Boston during the summer of 1987. Touring to support her smash first album, Whitney Houston, *the young star packed arenas all over the country.*

in the emotional wallop she can deliver when singing full blast."

At first, Whitney thought it was simply a matter of hard work paying off. After all, she had bided her time before concentrating on a music career, then spent two years recording her debut album. But she was becoming more than a big star; she was a phenomenon.

"As it went on—and it went *on*—I took a very humble attitude," she said. "I was not going to say, 'Hey, I sold 13 million records, check that out.' My mother always told me, 'Before the fall goeth pride.' "

Still, it was hard to stay humble when her hometown of Newark presented her with the key to the city soon after the Grammy ceremony. At the time, her father, John, was head of the city's planning board, which made the presentation all the more special. Furthermore, in May 1986, the readers of *People* magazine voted her "America's top new star." *Whitney Houston* spent a year in the top 10, including 14 weeks at number 1. "You Give Good Love," "Saving All My Love for You," "Greatest Love of All," and "How Will I Know" all went to number 1. Before that, Donna Summer, Olivia Newton-John, Cher, Roberta Flack, Brenda Lee, and Connie Francis were the only female artists with back-to-back number 1 songs. Now Whitney had scored four consecutive number 1 singles.

Even though Whitney was determined not to let fame change her, it was hard to keep it from changing the way her friends treated her. "They no longer call me Nippy, but *Whitney*," she said. "When I go to visit I'm treated like some kind of goddess. I'm the same kind of girl I was five years ago, with the same morals and values. I do have a lot more money, and I'm a lot busier, but that's basically it."

"I'm proud of the way she handles herself," said John Houston. "When she's onstage she belongs to the audience, but 15 minutes after she's off, she's my kid again!"

But maybe she hadn't really gotten much opportunity to be a "kid." John later remembered a poignant moment during another tour through Europe in 1986. Many of the members of the tour went dancing after a concert in London, and John was amazed at Whitney's sudden burst of energy.

"Guess what, Daddy," she said, bounding up to him. "I've been dancing."

"And she proceeds to dance until four in the morning," John said later. "I almost cried, realizing that for three years she hadn't had the chance to act like a teenager."

Whitney's public image played on her youth. Davis had sold her as an elegant model on the cover of her debut album, but in the video for "How Will I Know" she danced and prowled in a panther-lean metallic dress. (The video also paid a nice little tribute to Aretha Franklin, who appeared briefly as a source of inspiration for Whitney.) She also brought unbelievable energy to a TV ad campaign for Diet Coke. Whitney was becoming the very image of young America, but there were times when that image was just too perfect to live up to.

Whitney tried to control what the public saw. While singers like Madonna were vamping it up, she kept her public image clean and cool. "I don't think women are made to do anything they don't want to do," she said. "Women have a clear choice. That's the way I was raised. My mother always said to me, 'If you want to be respected, act with respect. If you don't, then you'll be disrespected.' "

She had also graduated to such a level of celebrity that she was known by her first name alone: Whitney. So she and Davis decided to make her first name the title of her follow-up album. Public anticipation mounted, and as an old industry pro, Davis knew that it could be hard to duplicate a

Whitney at the 1988 American Music Awards with her mother, Cissy, and her brother Gary (right). Throughout the highs and lows of her career, Whitney has remained close to her family, drawing comfort and support from them.

debut's success on a sophomore effort. Whitney had had two years to prepare her debut, and then another year to watch its success grow. Now she had to start all over again.

"My voice, in a lot of ways, has grown since I recorded the album two years ago," she said at the time. "It's gotten a lot more—soulful. There's a lot more grit to it now."

Again, a group of producers worked with Whitney, but this time Narada Michael Walden got the lion's share of the songs. Walden, who hailed the singer as the product of "vocal royalty," brought out the best in the lively, up-tempo Whitney that appealed to young listeners. From the leadoff cut and first single, the driving "I Wanna Dance with Somebody (Who Loves Me)," *Whitney* was a hit. It entered the charts at number 1, making it the first single by a woman ever to do so. When "So Emotional," "Love Will Save the Day," and "Where Do Broken Hearts Go" all followed the first single to the top of the charts, Whitney broke the record for most consecutive number 1 singles, previously held only by the Beatles and the Bee Gees.

Whitney now had a track record and a position to defend in the industry, and some critics found that she wasn't quite living up to their great expectations. *Newsweek*, in an article entitled "The Selling of Whitney Houston," called *Whitney* "a megadisappointment." The article continued, "It is unadventurous the way it uses Whitney's powers, and most of its songs are stupefyingly banal. There's no real sweat. . . .The problem is that when all the songs she belts out are about passion, she still sounds underneath like a girl who never stayed out past curfew."

Today, some of that criticism of *Whitney* seems valid, even if *Newsweek* did put it somewhat harshly. Walden gets the album off to a percolating, polyrhythmic start with "I Wanna Dance with Somebody (Who Loves Me)," wherein the listener can hear Whitney trying out new vocal effects and tricks. But that's just the problem, according to some critics: the listener can hear her trying. The second cut, "Just the Lonely Talking Again," has a chatty set of lyrics and a demanding melody that Whitney sings too crisply, too pitch-perfect, so that when she gets to the lines "It's the second time around/for you and I, boy/and believe me it's confusing me," she doesn't honestly project the weariness the song suggests. Madonna producer Jellybean Benitez contributes the cooking "Love Will Save the Day," but the lyric lines are so long and demanding that they don't give Whitney much room to add the vocal embellishments of traditional soul and gospel singing that she excels at. "Didn't

We Almost Have It All" is a Michael Masser ballad, with Whitney's singing again so precise that it reflects none of the worldly regret implied in the title. Walden then returns with the up-tempo "So Emotional," with Whitney double-tracking her vocals—singing background for herself—for added urgency.

On the ballad "Where You Are," producer Kashif overwhelms Whitney's voice with rattlesnake percussion, and Vincent Henry's laughing saxophone completely breaks the mood. Walden's "Love Is a Contact Sport" gets off to a silly start with the background singers chanting, "Contact!" Masser and Gerry Goffin reunite for "You're Still My Man," and the certainty and conviction required by the song suit Whitney perfectly, but again the melody too blatantly shows off her three-octave range.

Finally, on "For the Love of You," the Isley Brothers supply a song that's meant to be sung, not read as sheet music, and Whitney stretches out delightfully in the chorus, hinting at the more relaxed singing style she would eventually develop. "Where Do Broken Hearts Go" truly is as banal as the title, but then the album finishes with "I Know Him So Well," a triumphant duet with Cissy that seems to be about John Houston. "I'd really like to record with my mother," Whitney had said in the early days of her career. "She is my teacher, my adviser—she's my greatest inspiration." Now she finally had.

Time magazine, in a more respectful article than *Newsweek*'s, said, "*Whitney* marks graduation day for the prom queen of soul." The piece placed Whitney at the forefront of what was at that time a renaissance of female pop elegance, reflected in Dionne Warwick's revival of the Bacharach song "That's What Friends Are For," Aretha and George Michael's single "I Knew You Were Waiting for

Me," and Barbra Streisand's *The Broadway Album*, as well as the rise of new artists like Sade and Anita Baker.

But this abundance of female pop talent only served to make some writers demand more from Whitney. Some said she was a media creation of Clive Davis. "Anytime anybody gets this big, it's the result of timing as well as talent as well as luck as well as a promotional push," said *Billboard* magazine columnist Paul Grein. That touched a nerve with Whitney. "I don't like it when they see me as this little person who doesn't know what to do with herself—like I have no idea what I want, like I'm just a puppet and Clive's got the strings," she said. "That's demeaning to me, because that isn't how it is, and it never was. And never will be."

According to newspaper reports, Whitney earned a staggering $44 million in 1987—less than Madonna's $47 million, but still more than Michael Jackson, who earned $43 million. "Now, money is important," Whitney admitted, "but the things that really matter are the art and love for what you are doing."

How did she maintain her sense of perspective? "I do it by prayer," she said. "I believe in God the Almighty. My parents raised me in such a way that I don't have to do all those things that others are doing around me."

She took home her second consecutive Grammy for Best Pop Vocal Performance by a Female in 1987. Whitney was at the top of her field. But with all that popularity came a lot of pressure. A few critics had long found fault with Whitney: her voice was so clear and pure and her singing so seemingly effortless that they suspected she wasn't giving it her all. And in concert she sometimes tended to let the show drag and just rely on her voice to carry her performance. Whitney made no apologies. "God gave me a voice to sing with," she said, "and when you have that what other gimmick is there?"

But as 1987 rolled into 1988 the pressure began to show. Whitney would arrive late for performances, then take the stage without so much as an apology. She was sought out for a movie version of the life of Josephine Baker, a talented and charismatic African-American singer and dancer who had found success in Europe before blacks had experienced anything approaching equality in the American entertainment business. But Whitney turned down the role. Then she was pegged to star in the movie version of *Dreamgirls*, a Broadway musical loosely based on the story of Diana Ross and the Supremes, but eventually she backed out.

"Everybody thought of me doing it because it was so obvious," Whitney said. "You want somebody who can sing and be a 'Dreamgirl,' get Whitney. But that's why I didn't want to do it—it's too obvious."

Whitney retreated to a new multimillion-dollar estate in rural New Jersey. She made $45 million in 1988, but people kept clamoring for more—another album, an attempt at movies, more contact with her fans, more acknowledgment that she was an African-American artist struggling with African-American issues. It was all too much for her and it showed.

In 1989, Whitney won a Soul Train Music Award for Best Album by a Female Vocalist, but as she made her way to the stage to accept it, some people booed. A few even called her an "Oreo"—black on the outside, white on the inside.

Whitney tried to understand this hurtful outburst. "My success happened so quickly that when I first came out, black people felt, 'She belongs to us,'" Whitney said. "And then all of a sudden the big success came and they felt I wasn't theirs anymore, that I wasn't within their reach. It was felt that I was making myself more accessible to whites, but I wasn't."

Stardom was rapidly proving to be more difficult than Whitney had ever imagined.

5

ALL THE MAN THAT
I NEED

❦

Living in the spotlight and always having to act the part of the perfect young woman was getting to Whitney. "Picture this," she said. "You wake up every day with a magnifying glass over you. Someone always is looking for something—somebody, somewhere is speaking your name every five seconds of the day, whether it's positive or negative." In many ways, she felt that she had become a commodity, a thing rather than a person. "Like my friend Michael [Jackson] says, 'You want our blood but you don't want our pain,'" Whitney observed. "I had to catch up on all that Whitney Houston had become. It just took off so fast that I had to backtrack."

In times of trouble, Whitney Houston has always sought solace from within her family. "Family's very important to Whitney," said Deborah Schindler, a movie producer who worked with her on *Waiting to Exhale*. "She surrounds herself with people who are protective of her, a comfort zone."

"When I first started out, I juiced my mother," Whitney remembered. "I was like, 'Ma, Ma, Ma, Ma, Ma, what do I do? What do I say? How do I handle it?' Now, I know. You learn, you grow up, and you become your own woman. But we're still very close. When other people are talking [trash], I know my mother won't blow smoke . . . and I know she'll tell me the truth. She's honest with me."

Whitney clowns around with Bobby Brown following one of her performances at Radio City Music Hall in New York.

Whitney's love for children is evident during this 1991 Christmas Party sponsored by the Whitney Houston Foundation for Children, which she founded in 1989.

Likewise, she called on her father to take over her business affairs in Nippy, Inc. "First of all I was in trouble," Whitney explained,

and I knew that my father is a very wise man, a smart man. I figured that if there is anybody I can trust, it is my daddy, because I know my daddy loves me. And I know that before the business and the money came, it was just him and family. Plus, my mom was on Daddy's case to get involved in my business.

And besides that fact, my father has a good business mind. I just feel comfortable with him being there. I feel secure that somebody is watching over me, and watching over everybody else, too. I trust him. He literally came in and saw the troubled areas and what needed to be done, what I needed to do, and we did it.

"After that first year, there were some misconceptions about Whitney," John Houston said. "Some people felt that she was syrupy, that she had no social awareness, that she was a Barbie Doll. That is not the case. She is well-informed, politically aware, smart and articulate, and in the final analysis she runs the show."

Few people knew, for instance, that Whitney was an avid contributor of both time and money to various charities: the United Negro College Fund, AIDS research, and Habilitative Systems, Inc. in Chicago. In 1989, she developed the Whitney Houston Foundation for Children. "It supports children of all ages," Whitney said, "anywhere I can help—whether it's an abuse situation or a child with AIDS or a mother who needs help taking care of her children. I love kids. I've always had a concern for young people."

"It's her career, her money, and nobody makes decisions but her," John said in summing up his business role. "She's not into the routine of running the office day-to-day. I'm paid to do that."

Her family gave her security. But sometimes that security was a mixed blessing. "Your family can really get on your nerves," Whitney later admitted in a playful moment, "and they know they can get on your nerves. So I get mad. I fire everybody, then hire them back.

"You see, everything else in the world can be wrong with me, but my family has to be right or nothing will be right with me.

"I've also learned that problems don't change, no matter if you have millions, billions, or zillions. You've still got problems." But her family gave her a buffer zone so that she could better deal with those problems.

In 1990, Whitney emerged with a new album, *I'm Your Baby Tonight*. She appeared on the cover looking typically spunky, in a loose-fitting sweatshirt, trim pants, and sprightly white tennies. But she was also posed sitting on a motorcycle bearing the license plate NIPPY, her father's old nickname for her. The music showed this effort to balance the new with the old. Whitney didn't turn completely away from ballads, but she did include more up-tempo numbers. Narada Michael Walden returned to handle 3 of the album's 11 songs, and the hot production team of L. A. Reid and Kenneth "Babyface" Edmonds did four, including the title song. Michael Masser again gave her a tender ballad, "After We Make Love," but she also produced a song herself, the final number "I'm Knockin'." She was also joined by a couple of music titans: Stevie Wonder produced the duet "We Didn't Know" and joined her on the vocals, and Luther Vandross produced "Who Do You Love."

I'm Your Baby Tonight captures Whitney in a transitional stage in her career. The title song leads off the album, with Reid and Edmonds displaying a more relaxed and assured sense of funk than Walden ever did. They double- and triple-tracked Whitney's vocals, building a rhythmic momentum reminiscent of Michael Jackson's work. The next cut, "My Name Is Not Susan," finds Whitney biting off the lines of the chorus in an effective manner. Walden then produces a fine ballad in "All the Man That I Need," with a simple yet inspirational melody that gives Whitney plenty of room to maneuver, especially in the verses. Kenny G provides an undistinguished sax solo at the break before the song builds to a crescendo with a gospel chorus in the background.

But then comes the bland, Walden-produced ballad "Lover for Life," which asks the ridiculous musical question, "Will you sentence me to be your lover for life?" Reid and Edmonds get the album back on track with "Anymore," with Whitney again adopting a Michael Jackson-style rhythm toward the end. Their next ballad, "Miracle," finds Whitney a little too restrained, especially given the darker elements of the lyrics, but she rises to the occasion to end the song triumphantly. In Walden's "I Belong to You," however, Whitney fails to achieve emotional depth when she sings of how she's "been to the bottom." She makes a lovely entrance to Vandross's "Who Do You Love," and Cissy chimes in with some nice background vocals, but the song fails to progress beyond where it goes in the first 30 seconds. Whitney has better results on "We Didn't Know," with Stevie Wonder providing a slinky rhythm; there are times when their singing is so together that it's tough to tell where one leaves off and the other picks up the melody. Masser and Goffin again reunite on "After We Make Love," but this song lacks their usual magic. Whitney closes things out with her own production, "I'm Knockin'."

In spite of its ups and downs, *I'm Your Baby Tonight* was an impressive album. Still, it met with some resistance from her old fans. Some of them wanted Whitney to stay frozen in time as a youthful, gorgeous ingenue. In the end, *I'm Your Baby Tonight* sold "only" seven million copies.

Disappointing sales for her third album were accompanied by an increasingly confrontational relationship with the media. "They're devils to me," she would later declare, "and they're out to eat my flesh." When an entertainer achieves superstardom as Whitney had, she can expect to read sensationalistic lies and half-truths about herself in the supermarket tabloids. However, Whitney also grew irritated with the way that even supposedly reputable newspapers, magazines, and TV news shows concentrated on her every move.

And it wasn't just the "white" newspapers and magazines of the mainstream media that were focusing on Whitney. Playing on the title of Janet Jackson's *Rhythm Nation* album, black comedian Keenan Ivory Wayans did a skit about "Whitney Houston's Rhythmless Nation" on the Fox TV network's variety program *In Living Color*. In many ways, that sketch stung even more than the ridiculous rumors printed in the tabloids. "Don't say I don't have soul or what you consider to be 'blackness,'" Whitney shot back. "I know what my color is. I was raised in a black community with black people, so that has never been a thing with me."

She had a brief fling with Eddie Murphy. They had a lot in common, as they were both big stars with humble roots in New Jersey. Their relationship set off a media feeding frenzy, and some of the trashier tabloids even insisted that she was pregnant by Murphy.

She and Murphy were "just two very friendly people," she said, "the kind of friends who don't really have a got-to-see-you, got-to-have-you kind of relationship. Because of my career and his career—I'm here and he's there, he's there and I'm here—it's hard to establish a relationship. Even when you have two people who have the money, the fame and the same kind of status. It's the time factor—having the time to establish a relationship and to try to keep it."

The public scrutiny could not have done much to help matters. "It's really strange," Whitney said. "Michael Jackson said it best: You become this personality instead of a person. That's what's strange about this image business—the more popular you become, the weirder they want to make you."

Whitney was particularly irked by rumors concerning her sexuality. In her early years of stardom, she had typically rebuffed men who asked her out. She knew that being rich and famous and beautiful made her a target for people seeking to take advantage of her. "I just never wanted to be married," she said. "I had an independence that didn't include

Whitney's brief relationship with actor Eddie Murphy sparked intense media attention and rumors that she was carrying his child. "You become this personality instead of a person," she said of the public scrutiny. "The more popular you become, the weirder they want to make you."

marriage." But some people speculated that Whitney was actually enjoying a sexual relationship with her childhood friend Robyn Crawford.

Whitney and Robyn had been friends since meeting at summer camp while teenagers. When Whitney became famous, she hired Robyn as her assistant—a role she retains to this day—and they were roommates for a while. Most people probably wouldn't think twice about two young women who were childhood friends sharing an apartment in a city as they embarked on their professional careers. But for Whitney, it became just another curious detail that aroused speculation.

"I realize that this thing has been fueled by the fact that I'm very private with my life. I don't make it my business to expose my relationships. It's hard enough to keep just one," she said. "I've had boyfriends all my life. . . . And I've had great relationships. But I've never been one to have five relationships at the same time. . . . You know, I was raised as a Christian, and my mother was very strict with me as far as boys were concerned. She told me that the way to a man's heart is [to] . . . let him get to know you first.

"I don't want to *fall* in love," she said. "I want to *walk in* and find out what I'm loving. I don't want to get hurt. Nobody does."

Regardless of whether Whitney was dating, she and Robyn had always been close friends. As a teenager, "I didn't like to fight," Whitney said. "I was not outspoken and really outgoing. Robyn was. [The other girls] always wanted to whip me for no reason. So once Robyn became my big sister, all that ended.

"People want to know if there is a relationship," Whitney added. "Our relationship is that we're friends. We've been friends since we were kids. She is now my employee. I'm her employer. And we're still best of friends. That's what it is."

The more cynical members of the media suggested that Whitney was just covering up her lesbian affair by dating Eddie Murphy. Their relationship eventually cracked under the strain of their demanding careers and stardom. But another man had caught Whitney's eye.

Whitney had met Bobby Brown at the 1989 Soul Train Music Awards. It was a bright spot in that dark evening during which she had been booed. "He was kicking 'Don't Be Cruel,'" his hit single at the time, Whitney later explained. "He was hot, he was on fire." Whitney and Robyn were sitting with their good friends, the famous gospel singers BeBe and CeCe Winans, who just happened to be seated behind Bobby and his entourage. Whitney was feeling mischievous. She started annoying Bobby by playfully tapping him on the back of the head.

"Whitney, if you keep hitting Bobby, he's going to be mad at you," Robyn said.

So Whitney leaned forward and said sweetly, "Bobby, I'm so sorry."

Bobby turned around. "Yeah, well just don't let it happen again," he said.

"And I was like, 'Ooh, this guy doesn't like me,'" Whitney said later on. "Well, I always get curious when somebody doesn't like me. I want to know why." So she surprised everyone by inviting him to her 26th birthday party that summer, and he surprised everyone by accepting her invitation. A few months after that, they met again at a Winans concert.

"After the show, CeCe had a party and we all went out to dinner," Whitney said. "At the end of the dinner, Bobby walked up to me and said, 'If I asked you to go out with me, would you?' At the time, I was dating someone, but it was kind of—eh. So I said, 'Yeah, I would.' And he said, 'You really would?'—he's so cool—'I'll pick you up tomorrow at eight.' And we've been friends ever since. See, our whole relationship started out as friends. We'd have dinner, laugh, talk, and go home. It wasn't intimate. And then it kind of dawned on us, 'What's going on here?'"

Many people in the media thought they made an odd couple. For one thing, Whitney was six years older than he was. And while she was known for her sophisticated pop sound, he was at the height of the hip-hop craze, teaming with producer Teddy Riley on the dance single "Don't Be Cruel." But they actually had a great deal in common. Whitney had not exactly grown up rich in New Jersey, and Bobby had grown up in the rough Orchard Park projects of Boston. Although Whitney was older, Bobby had actually been a star longer, starting out

Whitney's soul-stirring rendition of "The Star-Spangled Banner" during the 1991 Super Bowl became a big hit. Over $500,000 in profits from the single were donated to the American Red Cross.

with the teen group New Edition, which first hit the charts in 1983 with "Candy Girl." He had since gone on to a successful solo career beginning with "My Prerogative." What Whitney liked most about him was that he treated her as an equal: he wasn't intimidated by her stardom, as were so many other guys she had dated.

If her romance with Bobby didn't put the rumors to rest, Whitney's comments did. "Robyn is my best friend, who knows me better than any woman has ever known me," she said. "We have been tight for years, but when I met Bobby, Robyn and I had had enough time together. We used to be roommates, but now . . . she [has] moved into her own place, about thirty minutes away."

As the relationship between Whitney and Bobby grew, she began 1991 on a high note. She was scheduled to sing the national anthem at Super Bowl XXV. At the same time, the United States brimmed with patriotism from the Persian Gulf War against Iraq. When Whitney nailed "The Star-Spangled Banner" with one of her most heart-felt performances, it created a sensation. The performance was issued as a single and immediately went gold. "My timing was right with it," Whitney shrugged. Yet again, cynics in the media questioned how Clive Davis had been ready with high-tech mobile recording facilities to get the performance down on tape. But more than $500,000 in profits from the single were donated to the American Red Cross Gulf Crisis Fund and the Whitney Houston Foundation for Children. And Whitney performed for about 3,000 returning Gulf War veterans and their families that March. That concert became the HBO special "Welcome Home Heroes with Whitney Houston." In many ways, Whitney had never been more popular.

6

HOLLYWOOD

The year 1991 would be one of intense highs and lows for Whitney. She went on tour in support of *I'm Your Baby Tonight*, but at one of the first stops, in Lexington, Kentucky, she got involved in a fracas with unruly fans at her hotel. No formal charges were filed, but it was bad publicity for Whitney. She also suffered because of some erratic performances. Ticket sales were down, and some shows were even canceled because of the row in Kentucky.

That summer, Bobby Brown asked her to marry him. He had asked once before and Whitney had flatly turned him down, saying, "Forget about it, no way. It's just not in my plans." But over the course of the following year, things had changed between them. When Bobby asked again in September 1991—this time presenting a humble little ring—Whitney said yes. Then he whipped out a 10-carat diamond—the real engagement ring.

"He played me like Atari [the video game]," Whitney later said with a smile.

Still, it was a stressful time. At the end of the year Whitney had to endure snickers from the media when her father, John, married her former housekeeper, Peggy Griffith. But that proved a minor stress in comparison with a real pressure cooker that year: at last, Whitney was preparing for her first movie role.

Whitney and Bobby on their wedding day in the summer of 1992.

Years earlier, Hollywood star Kevin Costner had bought the rights to a script called *The Bodyguard*. It concerned a love relationship that developed between a bodyguard and the singing star he was assigned to protect. Costner had immediately thought of Whitney for the part. "There are certain singers that occupy that territory that includes a world-class voice, real elegance and a physical presence," he said. "Diana Ross and Barbra Streisand are two. Whitney Houston is another."

Costner's decision to hire Whitney had little to do with race. Thirty, 20, or even 10 years earlier, the very notion of an interracial romance would have been the most controversial aspect of the movie. Yet Costner never concerned himself with that, and in the end the film simply accepts the two major characters on their own terms. For him, it was the story of two professionals from different environments who stumble into an unlikely romance. "I don't think race is an issue here," he said. "The film is about a relationship between two people, and it would have been a failure if it became a film about interracial relationships.

"Some of my choices are real simple," he added, "and it's very easy to fall in love with Whitney."

Although Whitney ultimately accepted the film role, she was undeniably intimidated at the prospect of playing a lead role with an established actor. "I wanted to do some acting," she said, "but, I mean, I never thought I'd be co-starring with Kevin Costner!" At first, Whitney's busy concert schedule delayed production. Then she deliberately kept her schedule busy so that she could continue to put it off. "I was scared," Whitney admitted. "It took me two years to decide to do it." Finally, Costner needed to know: Was she in or was she out? After getting Costner to promise that he would lead her through it, she was in. She cleared the early part of 1992 for filming.

"I promised her two things," Costner said, "that I would be right there with her, and she would not be bad, because I refuse to let anybody fail around me." He also convinced her not to take any sort of acting lessons; he wanted her "natural" and "charming," not studied and contrived.

"It's a different level, a whole new facet of entertainment," Whitney said about the experience. "While music has a rhythm that comes naturally to me, acting takes concentration. I would compare it with starting my music career and working the clubs. It was like starting all over again, but in a new field."

As if making her Hollywood debut and planning a wedding weren't pressure enough, Whitney found out before shooting began that she was pregnant with Bobby's child. When she suffered a

Whitney's first movie role was actress/singer Rachel Marron in The Bodyguard. *Some viewers felt that the character was very similar to Whitney herself.*

miscarriage during production, word leaked out in the media. "People don't realize—though they should—how stress will tear you down, how it will wear out your body," Whitney said. "I was giving just so much to this film role, and I went right from the concert tour to filming. My body was not ready to carry a child. I think it was God's way of saying, 'This is not right this time, let's try it another time.' "

Again, some people saw an opportunity to sensationalize Whitney's life with Bobby. But she kept working on the movie, and the loss actually brought her and Bobby closer together.

"I was scared," Whitney said. "I was really nervous. It was a new plateau. It was a lot of hard, intense work. And there were moments when I thought, 'I can't do this.' And Bobby would say, 'Yes you can. You can do it. And you're gonna do it.' There were days I'd get up in the morning and say, 'I can't take this anymore.' And he'd say, 'Yes, you can. Come on, girl, get up. Come on.' You know? He's a motivator. At moments like that you remember what somebody means to you."

That summer, when filming was done, Whitney and Bobby got married at her New Jersey mansion. Both bride and groom wore white, and Whitney's French-lace dress cost $40,000. John Houston walked her down the aisle; Robyn Crawford was the maid of honor. The 17-piece New York Metropolitan Opera Orchestra played the wedding march. About 800 people attended. "I think they're the couple of the century," said Bobby's former New Edition producer Maurice Starr.

"I may be a bad boy and she may be America's sweetheart, but it's love," Bobby said. "When it happens, you have to grab it. You can't let it go no matter what anybody else thinks. Whitney is a proud black woman. That's what really drew me to her. She's beautiful, not just outside, but on the inside."

On his 1992 album *Bobby,* they performed a

duet called "Something in Common." On the liner notes, Bobby dedicated it to "all those who don't believe in love, especially ours."

Post-production work on *The Bodyguard* dragged on. Costner, true to his promise of perfection, called Whitney out to Hollywood to re-record some of her lines. He was going to make sure everything was as good as possible. "It was really nice, really a joy to work with Kevin, and it had a lot to do with his personality," Whitney said. "He is down-to-earth. He doesn't trip. He's into his work. And he's very kind, he's effective, and he's considerate."

It was already obvious that they had something special on their hands. Costner had chosen an old Dolly Parton song, "I Will Always Love You," as the movie's showcase number, and Whitney turned it into a tour de force. When she was through recording it, she knew she had nailed it.

Today, "I Will Always Love You" remains one of Whitney's greatest performances, the place where her technique and passion finally lock into the subject matter of a great song. She opens the song singing a cappella, her voice restrained but also impassioned. Then, in the chorus, she cuts loose with full-throated abandon—like the panther choosing that moment to pounce. There are no empty vocal pyrotechnics; everything is done to effect and in proportion. Toward the end, just when a listener thinks she has wrung everything she can out of the song, it modulates into a higher key for the final chorus and Whitney swings up to that higher level with ease and confidence. She projects yearning, regret, but more than that the power of pure endurance. In many ways, it was the performance of a lifetime.

Producer David Foster's minimal backing music plays a big part in the power of "I Will Always Love You": it is addition by subtraction, giving Whitney room to fill up the speakers. But after that, Foster's

Whitney and costar Kevin Costner, who helped her through her first acting experience. The Bodyguard was incredibly successful, with over $400 million in ticket sales worldwide.

contributions to *The Bodyguard*'s soundtrack come up short. Whitney has to carry "I Have Nothing," and she can only do so much; in the end, the lack of support from the backing musicians is too much, and she winds up straining for effect. The delicate ending she arrives at has the same impact as a dollop of whipped cream on a raw steak. Narada Michael Walden returns to the fold to produce "I'm Every Woman," Whitney's remake of the old Chaka Khan cut, which was originally written by Nickolas Ashford and Valerie Simpson. But it's mix masters Robert Clivilles and David Cole, the producers behind the C+C Music Factory, who really get the song percolating with the addition of shuffle-step rhythmic percussion. Whitney has little of Chaka's abandon, but she exults in the song before invoking Chaka's name at the end with a giddy laugh. "Run to You" is another tame Foster production, although it finds Whitney working on the lower register of her voice—a deep, rich timbre—with good results. "Queen of the Night" is a thumping metallic funk number, an L. A. Reid and Babyface Edmonds production, quite uncharacteristic of Whitney, but perfectly fitting with Rachel, her character in the movie. The tune gives the impression that Whitney was letting a little of her "raunchy" side show under the guise of playing a part. Whitney ends her contributions to *The Bodyguard* soundtrack with a tender version of the childhood hymn "Jesus Loves Me," with BeBe Winans adding background vocals and some extra lyrics, as well as coproducing the song with Whitney.

The release of the movie and the soundtrack album were timed to create maximum interest, and when "I Will Always Love You" hit, it was an instant smash. It went to number 1 and stayed there for a record 14 weeks, becoming the largest-selling commercial single in history. The album went on to sell 33 million copies worldwide, making it the biggest-selling soundtrack in history.

If Whitney thought her debut album had continued to sell for a long time, she hadn't seen anything yet. "I Will Always Love You" created a worldwide sensation, to the point where some people began to get positively annoyed. Two incidents in England were so comical that they attracted attention in the United States. One 31-year-old mother of two children in Kensington, England, grew so enraged because her neighbors played the song over and over that she stormed into their apartment and tossed the stereo and the speakers out the window. "It was driving us all up the wall," she told reporters. "I had just had enough." And a 20-year-old woman in Middlebrough County was sentenced to seven days in jail after her repeated high-volume playing of the song caused her neighbors to complain of psychological torture; police cited her for noise pollution.

The *New York Times* mentioned those incidents in a story with the headline "A Love Song that Some Love to Hate," going on to quote local sources, such as a 19-year-old New York City record store employee who said, "I just can't stand the song. I think Whitney Houston has a good voice, but it all depends on what a song does for a person. For me, it got annoying, really annoying."

"The bottom line is that people like songs that have a lot of meaning and emotion in them," said one New York City radio executive, "and this song has an incredible amount of emotions."

"I like Whitney Houston's sense of legato [smooth connection between notes]," summed up one music consumer. "It was a great song. But there's only so much you can take."

Whitney took it all in stride, admitting that sometimes she looked at all her exposure in magazines and newspapers, on TV and radio, and said, "God, I'm sick of myself."

Where the movie itself was concerned, some critics took issue with her acting, and it's true that there were some spots in the film where she appeared stiff. Even when other critics cheered her performance, they sometimes speculated that it was authentic only because the demanding, exasperating pop diva in the movie probably mirrored Whitney in real life. But there was no denying the overall success of the music and the movie. The film's ticket sales reached over $400 million worldwide.

And, while her role may have confirmed the feelings of those who already thought she was a spoiled diva, it also sustained her reputation for being someone with a sense of restraint and responsibility. In an era when sex and violence ruled in Hollywood, there were no nude scenes in *The Body-*

guard. "The movie was meant to be tasteful," Whitney said. "It wasn't about having sex and acting crazy. And whatever I do, I'm not going to incriminate myself in any way. It wasn't required that I have to take off my clothes. It's a film with integrity."

By way of contrast, she could compare her wholesome image with Bobby's sexually provocative persona. "I look at Bobby's videos and I go, 'Oh, honey, God!' " Whitney said. "But I know that that person in the video is my husband and he comes home to me. He loves me. And that," she added, "is his business, and that's what he does for a living. That's part of his entertainment, his career." Whitney had long since figured out the difference between image and reality, and she knew the importance of exerting a certain amount of control over what the public saw.

It may not have been a smooth ride, but Whitney had made the transition to Hollywood star.

7

WAITING TO EXHALE

✿

On March 4, 1993, Whitney's life again changed dramatically. Whitney gave birth to six-pound, twelve-ounce Bobbi Kristina Houston Brown at the St. Barnabas Medical Center in Livingston, New Jersey.

Some women don't take to pregnancy; Whitney did. "I loved every moment of it," she said. "I had the best time. And I think a lot of it was due to Bobby because he was such a charmer. He was the best friend and the best husband. There was nothing he wouldn't do for me."

Apparently, a large part of Bobby's job was responding to her cravings: "I have to have a submarine every now and then," Whitney said, referring to her favorite turkey and cheese sandwiches. "And potato chips and ice cream," she added.

Her mother and other members of her family were there for her, too. "Having a child is like a whole new world, a whole new thing," Whitney said. "My mother said to me when I was a child, 'You'll understand better when you have your own.' And I do. I understand the concern, the responsibility of having a child. There are a lot of joys and a lot of worries.

"I've never found anything more fulfilling than being a mother," she added. "I never thought that I could worry as much. . . . I worried when she was

Whitney shows off her daughter, Bobbi Kristina, at the 1994 American Music Awards.

inside of me, and I worry more now that she's out of me. She teaches me about love every day."

Whitney also got some strong support from longtime friend CeCe Winans, who agreed to become Bobbi Kristina's godmother. The two had become almost instantly close when they first met several years earlier.

"When we first met," Whitney remembered, "we would call each other and say, 'You know, I can't believe I miss you. Why am I missing you? I haven't known you that long.' CeCe and I are alike in a lot of ways."

The months it took between filming and final work on *The Bodyguard* had granted Whitney a natural breather, a time for her to concentrate on her baby and nothing else. But she already knew that wouldn't last forever. Five months after Bobbi Kristina was born, Whitney went on tour in support of *The Bodyguard* soundtrack.

Again, Whitney was dogged by reports of petulant performances. In Miami, one newspaper reviewer reported that "Houston took the stage with an attitude that smelled like rotting fish. . . . Her behavior was tacky, unprofessional, arrogant, and beneath the dignity of a singer of her talent and stature." But even on nights when she was late for the show or less than personable, she could still deliver the goods.

But her priorities had changed. Now she focused on her family, or "the two B's," as she called Bobby and Bobbi Kristina. "Having Bobbi Kristina," she said, "I could never do anything that could top that." When asked what she wanted out of her life and her career, she said, "Really, it has nothing to do with business whatsoever. It's my family. To raise children, to raise decent human beings. To keep my husband happy. To keep him strong. Things of that nature. They are very simple things."

Although it had been released late in 1992, *The*

Bodyguard wasn't eligible for the Grammys until 1994. It was then that Whitney reaped a harvest of awards: "I Will Always Love You" was named Song of the Year, and it earned Whitney another Grammy for Best Female Pop Vocalist. The soundtrack was also named Album of the Year. Whitney barely slowed down to accept the honors. She again went back on tour, and although the tabloids hounded her with reports that her marriage was in trouble, at one performance she called Bobby up onstage and told him she was pregnant again.

"Marriage is a beautiful institution," Whitney said. She continued,

> People don't know Bobby because there hasn't been that much on Bobby except that Bobby is this sexy man who does all this bumping and grinding. But

Whitney poses with fellow award-winner David Foster at the 1994 Grammy Awards. Foster produced Whitney's album, I Will Always Love You.

> Bobby is a family man. Bobby loves his mother, loves his family. He goes out when he wants to hear music, when he wants to know what's happening. He comes home. I know where my husband is. I know what my husband does. There are certain things I don't go for and Bobby knows that. And there's stuff he doesn't go for. That's why we can be together, because we both have the same standards.

"I can't wait to have a little brother or sister for Bobbi Kris," she added. "We'd like to have three kids, and I hope this one will be a boy."

A month later, however, Whitney suffered another miscarriage. Yet she threw herself back into her work, going on tour to South Africa, where the world-renowned activist Nelson Mandela had recently been elected president. A three-week tour climaxed with "Whitney: The Concert for a New South Africa," which again was turned into an HBO special. Whitney confirmed her status as a superstar.

But the pace was too hectic and demanding to sustain for long. She came home planning to return to movies, but on her own timetable. She had bought the property behind her New Jersey estate, and she put in a playground for "B.K.," as she called her daughter, as well as a basketball court and a lap pool. She moved her home studio into a building on the new property. Reading through scripts that were waiting for her after she had settled in, she came across a movie treatment for *Waiting to Exhale*, Terry McMillan's novel about the lives of four African-American women. Whitney was a natural for one of the parts, an elegant but troubled woman named Savannah. "Savannah is me," Whitney said later. "She's very straightforward, she knows what she wants, and she goes for it."

She was joined in the cast by Angela Bassett, Loretta Devine, and Lela Rochon. Best of all, the director was well-known actor Forest Whitaker, who created a comfortable, creative mood on the set.

"He has such a peaceful demeanor," Whitney said. "And such a quiet temperament, very even all the time. When he got upset, he took long walks and then would come back. And I thought, 'This is a very special guy.' "

"Working with this story and these performers is a filmmaker's dream," Whitaker responded. "I have tremendous respect for Terry's work, and we have made sure we stayed true to her vision."

It was a delicate project, as McMillan well knew. "It's not a movie from the 'hood," she said. "These women are pretty much educated. It's about their self-esteem in terms of their survival and not just about survival itself, which is what African-American movies seem to be about these days."

Shooting began in the spring of 1995, and right away Whitney got support from her more experienced costars. "The night before shooting, the entire cast and crew got together at a local bowling alley," Whitney remembered. "I was first on the shooting schedule, and I remember telling Angela, Loretta, and Lela how nervous I was. Angela said, 'Just go in there and do it.' My sisters were most encouraging, and I won't ever forget that."

"It was a sisterhood immediately," Bassett said. "The four of us bonded. Whitney is a very special lady. I felt blessed to meet her and work with her and come to know her."

Almost immediately, Whitney herself was gushing with enthusiasm about the experience. "In just two weeks, Forest has taught me a lot about acting," she said. "In *The Bodyguard* I was just simply playing a character that I was familiar with because she and I had the same kind of world. With Savannah, it's more like me without the fame. She allows me to be a lot more like myself. The great thing about it is that I have three other beautiful ladies who arc all great actresses and whom I can play off."

Whitaker had told her that she didn't need to

take any acting classes. He wanted her performance to be natural and relaxed. "I think what Hollywood was looking for was me," Whitney said, "and I guess they got it—so they don't want me to be tainted in any way."

Still, she was learning just from watching the other actresses work. "Angela should get an Oscar nomination for this," Whitney said. "That girl is amazing. I don't sing a song the same way every night. Different emotions come into play. Watching Angela do that in acting with words helped me a lot."

Terry McMillan praised Whitney's performance. "She's going to be a really better actress when she starts seeing herself as an actress and not a singer who acts," she predicted after seeing Houston's portrayal of Savannah.

Whitney found acting gratifying, but she resisted the notoriety that came with another type of fame. "You can't really plan fame or what you'll do with it once you have it," she said. "Or how you'll handle it. Or how you'll feel about your audiences. Or how they'll feel about you. I just want to sing. I wish people would concentrate more on my singing than on my life and my so-called temper. It's my life, my person, my moods, and I don't choose to share each and every bit of it with the entire world. didn't ask for all of this, all this attention and invasion of privacy. They say it comes with the territory—well, I don't think it does. Nor do I think it should have to."

But there was no denying the fact that her voice placed Whitney at the center of attention. Originally, she was not going to contribute to the *Waiting to Exhale* soundtrack; Whitney was going to act and nothing else. But then she and other people involved with the picture realized they would be a missing a great opportunity. Whitney agreed to do a few songs for the album, which would be produced

by Babyface Edmonds, but she also wanted the soundtrack to be a showcase for great women singers.

"I wanted this to be an album of women with distinction," she said, "that you could say their first name but you don't have to say their last." Toni Braxton, Mary J. Blige, and Aretha Franklin, Whitney's own "Auntie Ree," all contributed tracks. But the big hit would prove to be Whitney's own "Exhale (Shoop, Shoop)," a slow groove that featured the most relaxed and assured singing of her career.

When Whitney saw the lyrics to "Exhale (Shoop, Shoop)," she thought that Edmonds, working by this time without his old partner L. A. Reid, must have lost his creative balance and, more than that, his mind. What were all those "shoop, shoops" about? But once Whitney and Babyface themselves laid down that soft yet solid foundation of "shoops"

Whitney with her costars from Waiting to Exhale. *From left to right: Loretta Devine, Houston, Angela Bassett, and Lela Rochon.*

in the song's background, Whitney could glide, soar, growl, and waver with total spontaneity on the lead vocals. Never before has Whitney projected such mastery, such offhand confidence. Many fans still consider the bravura performance of "I Will Always Love You" to be Whitney's best, but critics seem to prefer her work on "Exhale (Shoop, Shoop)." If it ever could have been said that Whitney had a great voice but little idea of how to use it, this song put a permanent end to that criticism. And its soothing quality fits perfectly with the mood and texture of the movie, which is about how four friends are there for one another in times of need. Whitney's other two contributions to the *Waiting to Exhale* sound-track are both marked by the same easy, offhand mastery that she displays in "Exhale (Shoop, Shoop). She gives a quiet, almost whispering perfor-mance on "Why Does it Hurt So Bad," showing off that rich, low timbre she had been working on at the time of *The Bodyguard* and using it to good effect. Then she closes the album with a song she had long been planning: a duet with CeCe Winans. From the opening measures to the closing exchange of "count on" trade-off riffs, it's hard to distinguish the two singers from one another. But what comes across most clearly is their almost unbounded fond-ness for singing with one another. The duet is an effective, ego-free performance by both singers.

When it came time to promote the film, a new, more assertive Whitney emerged in interviews with the major magazines and newspapers. She was ready to admit that she had had a difficult career at times. She was far from perfect; so was was her marriage with Bobby. But even if she was humbled, she was unbowed.

"People think I'm Miss Prissy Pooh-Pooh," she said, "but I'm not. I like to have fun. I can get down. . . . I was born in Newark, New Jersey, with two brothers and a very strong father. It made me tough—perhaps too tough." Whitney made herself seem more real—unbelievably talented to be sure, but also flawed and human.

When *Waiting to Exhale* was released late in 1995, it created a phenomenon few in Hollywood had expected. Women—especially African-American women—flocked to see the stories of four women who were representative of real life on the big screen. The week it was released, *Waiting to Exhale* was the most popular movie in theaters. Soon, women started organizing "Shoop, Shoop" parties to talk about the movie and about the men in their lives. Whitney had found that she could touch people as an actress as well as a singer.

The film, however, was snubbed only a few months later when Oscar nominations were announced. Many said it was because the Hollywood establishment was still slow to recognize the achievements of African Americans. "We were afraid, even when we were making the movie, that our work wouldn't be recognized at the Oscars," Whitney said. "We talked about it on the set a lot.

"No matter what, whether the Oscars nominate us or not, the people do. And I think that's really where it lies," Whitney continued, showing that she had her own sense of what truly mattered.

8
THE GREATEST LOVE
OF ALL

Whitney took a little time off before returning to work. "I don't do movies back-to-back," she said. "I don't want to do movies like that. It's not about doing movies for the sake of doing movies or because it's Hollywood and it's beautiful and glamorous. I want to do great work with great people, and that takes time. I pick and choose carefully what I do. Of course, I'm a lot more creative in my own element, which is music, because it's always been my first love."

But somebody else who prided himself on picking his projects and doing great work had her in mind for a movie. Denzel Washington was getting ready to do a remake of the Hollywood classic *The Bishop's Wife*, about an angel who comes to earth to help a church family and ends up falling in love with the wife of a clergyman. Washington planned to star as the angel; he also planned to place the story in a Baptist setting and give it an African-American flavor and a new title, *The Preacher's Wife*.

Whitney has used her star power to continue her commitments to causes that support children, African Americans, and the chronically ill. Here she poses in London's Hyde Park with choir members for Reach Out and Touch, an organization that supports people with HIV/AIDS.

But who would play the title character? "When somebody mentioned Whitney, I immediately said, 'Right,'" Washington said. "She had grown up in the church, it was a natural fit."

Whitney thought that her church choir background would help the film, too. "Yes, you understand what the music is all about," she said. "You understand what it takes to sing gospel and to live it the best you can. And it's not easy. You've got to come from that place to know what it's all about."

Filming on *The Preacher's Wife* started in January 1996, and Whitney proved to be more natural and relaxed than ever in front of the camera as the title character, Julia.

"Julia and I clicked right away," she said. "But she's more than just a loving mom and a wife. She cares about family values. She tries very, very hard to give back to the community. But she also gets angry. She gets ticked off. She's human. She has normal feelings, but she has to hold them back.

"I know the preacher's wife. I've watched one for years. I have watched my aunts and my mother, who was director of music. You know, it's about standards."

That feeling of a higher purpose was shared by Washington and others in the cast. "We felt that this film was about the community taking charge again and raising our children," Whitney said.

"Whitney is very talented and great to work with," said Washington, who is himself the son of a minister. "It's great working on this set. Everyone gets along so well."

Whitney had high praise for Washington as well, saying she considered him "an older brother."

"He's a gentleman, very funny, silly like me," she added. "He was very easy to work with. He's an old pro."

Supermarket tabloids dogged Whitney and Washington with vicious rumors about a sizzling

Whitney earned good reviews for her performance opposite Denzel Washington in the 1996 film The Preacher's Wife.

romance on the set. More people than ever recognized the stories as untruc, though. Both Washington and Whitney were committed to their families. Whitney and Bobby, in fact, seemed to have recently emerged intact from a tough time in their relationship.

Whitney had been the first to admit that Bobby had difficulty living in his wife's shadow. In many ways, he had put his career on hold while she went on tour and made the transition to movies. At the same time, their marriage was under intense scrutiny. Some members of the media called Bobby's music "raunchy," and as evidence of his unsavory character, they pointed to how he had fathered three children out of wedlock before marrying Whitney. Whitney accepted those children, but the

In 1995, the Whitney Houston Foundation for Children donated $110,000 to a hospital in Whitney's hometown to create a special pediatrics unit. Cissy Houston, who is president of the foundation, spoke at the dedication. She is pictured here with hospital CEO William Vasquez.

pressure got to the couple just the same. They separated for a time, during which many reports of Bobby's rowdy behavior in nightclubs emerged. The worst of these stories became public in September 1995, when on a visit to his old Roxbury neighborhood in Boston the car he was in—registered to Whitney as a gift for him—was fired upon. Bobby's bodyguard, who was engaged to Bobby's younger sister, was killed. At that point, Bobby seemed to realize his life was out of control. He went into an alcohol rehabilitation program and emerged before Christmas, which he spent with Whitney and Bobbi Kristina.

"The bottle is out of my life now," he said, "so everything is all good."

"You don't know what kind of man he is unless

you live with him and know him yourself," Whitney said in his defense. "Bobby is the energy side of me, and I'm the calm side of him, which works for us. I married the man I'm in love with, the person I can have fun with and be real with. This isn't a game."

Bobby embarked on a new project in early 1996, joining a New Edition reunion. It would prove to be a success, reigniting interest in his career. And to previous movie roles in *Ghostbusters II* and Mario Van Peebles's *Black Panther* he added a new role in *The Thin Line Between Love and Hate*, with Martin Lawrence.

"A lot of men are threatened by strong and powerful women," said Jamie Brown, publisher of the magazine *Sister 2 Sister*, "but not Bobby. He always supported Whitney. Against his managers' advice, he put his career on hold to tour with her and be there for her. She knows the private side to Bobby Brown, a side the public doesn't know."

Others were not so forgiving. "Whitney is not used to failure," said Danyel Smith, music editor for *Vibe* magazine. "She does not want her marriage to fail. She's used to making a decision and seeing it through. And the more the media or her friends say, 'You're crazy, he doesn't love you,' the more firmly this plants her feet in the ground, 'I'm going to succeed in this like I have in everything else.' I think, for Whitney, coming to terms with perceived failure is more difficult than dealing with her husband."

Everyone seemed to have an opinion on Whitney, and everyone seemed to want to share it with the world. In any case, Whitney and Bobby were learning to live with the relentless media attention. "It hasn't put a strain on our marriage," Whitney argued. "If they haven't broken us up by now, they aren't going to do it. What God has put together, let no man put asunder." Whitney had always defended Bobby. "I want this marriage to be a success, to last until the end of time—whenever that is," she said.

She also claimed that he had changed her life and even her career for the better.

"I've learned to be freer from Bobby," she said. "I've learned to be a little more loose. Not so contained, you know?

"I've got the most handsome man. I've got the sexiest man alive," she said. "Praise God, things are going well. He's healthy and strong. I'm healthy and strong. We're both working. Bobbi Kristina is growing up. My baby is great."

Still, stardom sometimes continued to be a hassle. Whitney had to get restraining orders against two different men who were stalking her. It left her with an eerie feeling after she had played a character with similar problems in *The Bodyguard*. "Yes, I've had people threaten me, but not to the degree of a Rachel Marron," she said. "Thank God, because that's crazy. And I hope that's where it stays—in the movie."

And while Whitney seemed to be winning more acceptance by talking plainly of her difficulties and stressing that she was just a person too, fans could still be too demanding at times. Late in 1996, she was also shocked by the publication of *Good Girl Bad Girl*, a tell-all book written by the friend of a former employee. She labeled it "a collection of lies," going on to say, "It's trash."

"Fame is a curious game," Whitney said. "It takes concentration and discipline. People get in and think, 'I can do whatever I want and spend money the way I want to spend it, treat people how I want to treat them.' My mother said, 'It doesn't go like that.'

"This is a stressful life," she added. "It takes a lot of time and energy. I don't want to be doing this like this when I'm old. I want to be sitting back and watching my kids and grandkids."

She saw others trapped in the fame game who would never get that chance. Not many people

knew it, but Whitney had become friends with gangsta rapper Tupac Shakur through the music industry. They had seen each other for what turned out to be the final time at a party for *Waiting to Exhale*. "Baby, you've got to promise me something," Whitney told him, "don't let them get you."

"I won't," Shakur said.

He was gunned down in 1996. "That was the last thing I ever said to him," Whitney later recalled, "and he didn't do it. It hurt my heart for him to die."

But, as Whitney grew more mature and more comfortable with fame—or at least with how to deal with it—her career improved correspondingly. *The Preacher's Wife* proved to be a hit. Some people had maintained that Whitney had just been playing

Whitney thrilling her audience at the 1994 American Music Awards, during which she won seven honors and an Award of Merit for "outstanding contributions to the musical entertainment of the American public."

herself—a stuck-up diva—in *The Bodyguard,* and that the same was true of her role in *Waiting to Exhale,* in which she played a good woman stuck with an awful man.

What could those detractors say about *The Preacher's Wife?* Critics commended her newfound talent for comedy, which was brought out by director Penny Marshall, former star of the TV series *Laverne & Shirley.* Whitney herself said she felt she had "progressed by leaps and bounds" as an actress. And, of course, again the soundtrack album was a smash.

The soundtrack gave Whitney a chance to reconnect with her gospel roots. "Gospel taught me to do a wide range of things," she said, "how to sing fast, how to sing slow, how to sing when the tempo changes in the middle of a song, how to sing four-part harmony without thinking about it. And how to sing without music, which is how you learn everything there is to know about music, in terms of your voice being the instrument, your feet being the drum, your hands being the tambourine."

Whitney had long been planning to record a gospel album, and *The Preacher's Wife* soundtrack gave her the opportunity. From the opening song, "I Believe in You and Me," the soundtrack album finds *Whitney* pouring out emotion with effortless grace. The attempts at perfection that marked her early recordings, such as *Whitney,* are long abandoned here; she simply lets it flow. She remakes the Annie Lennox Eurodisco song "Step by Step" for her second cut, putting lots of gospel grit into it and a sharp counterpoint vocal phrase at the end. For the rest of the album, *Whitney* really gets down to authentic gospel. The Georgia Mass Choir joins her on "Joy," and Whitney hums with pleasure from the opening bars, giving way to the unfettered gospel emotionalism she had long denied herself in the studio. Other gospel singers may have "bigger" voices, but few are as versatile and expressive as Whitney, as she goes on to stretch out with "Hold On, Help Is on the Way," the strolling "I Go to the Rock," and the heartfelt "I Love the Lord." Bobby Brown and his old New Edition bandmate Ralph Tresvant, along with Johnny Gill, join Whitney for the grinding, gospel-tinged "Somebody Bigger Than You and I." Then Babyface returns to produce the finger-snapping Diane Warren song "You Were Loved" and his own composition, "My Heart Is Calling," which features Whitney further developing the low end of her range. Then Whitney hits a more traditional note with "Who Would Imagine a King" and "He's All Over Me," before Cissy Houston steps in to take the lead on "The Lord Is My Shepherd." Whitney finally closes things out with "Joy to the World."

"This project was especially close to my heart," Whitney wrote in the liner notes. "My beginnings are in gospel music. This is where I'm most comfortable." The result was her most self-assured album to date.

Whitney even went on to welcome attention in instances where it raised awareness of causes she believed in; in that vein, she hosted the Nickelodeon cable TV channel's Kids' Choice Awards ceremony.

Whitney formed her own movie production company, aligned with the Walt Disney Company's Touchstone Pictures, and bought the rights to a biography of Dorothy Dandridge, a beautiful and immensely talented but troubled African-American star whose career spanned the 1940s to the 1960s. Whitney hoped to play the lead role herself as soon as she felt fully ready and confident as an actress. "I don't think I'm ready for that role," she said. "I don't think I'm skilled enough to handle her story." But the story would now be hers as soon as she felt up to the task.

Her own critical judgments aside, she found herself the top African-American actress in the film industry, and the popularity of her films was creating more work for other minority actresses. "This is definitely a surprise to me," Whitney laughed, "as I'm sure it is to a lot of other people. But it happened, and I accept it as a blessing, and I just hope it opens the doors for others. I mean, God bless Jada Pinkett, who came up to me and said, 'Girl, you don't know what you've done. You've opened the door that was shut.' "

But she also expected to carry on with her music. That and family would remain the constant elements of her life. *The Preacher's Wife* had earned her new respect and a $10 million paycheck, but music remained her career, and she had racked up some pretty impressive numbers over the years: close to 100 million albums sold worldwide, 19 American Music Awards, 7 NAACP Image Awards, 5 People's Choice Awards, 5 Soul Train Awards, a spot in the Soul Train Hall of Fame, 2 Emmys, and—last but not least—5 Grammys.

One day, Whitney was taken aback when a teenager interviewing her for *TV Guide* blurted out, "I've loved you since I was two!" In another interview she found herself being compared with Madonna as one of the elder stateswomen of pop music. Still, she said she felt comfortable with that. "Madonna and I certainly aren't in competition," she said. As for the other singers who came along— from Mariah Carey to Alanis Morissette, whose album *Jagged Little Pill* eventually broke the *Whitney Houston* record for sales of a debut album—Whitney said, "I've been out here since 1985, so whoever comes has to come *after* me."

In spite of the buffetings of fame, Whitney's family and friends remain close, and she again retreated into their comforting presence after she suffered another miscarriage early in 1997. She and

Bobby maintain that their marriage is still strong and that they'll continue to try for more children while balancing their careers. Robyn Crawford still works with her. Her father, John, runs Nippy, Inc., the business side of her holdings, and her mother, Cissy, runs the Whitney Houston Foundation for Children on the charity side.

"I like to deal with kids, probably more than I like to deal with some adults," Whitney explained. "Kids don't pass judgment on you, because they don't come with all that baggage we adults do. I don't know about being a role model. I have lots of roles. But if I can just inspire them to look at what I've done and say, 'Well, if I get my education, if I'm inspired by the right people, then I can do what she did.' "

In addition to offering her help and guidance to others, Whitney Houston now seems able to recognize the things that truly matter to her—and to pursue them wherever they take her. Whether she is singing, acting, or caring for her family, Whitney has decided that life is "not always about fame and fortune. It's about loving what you do. If you love what you do, and you inspire others to do great things, that's really worth it to me."

DISCOGRAPHY

Whiney Houston   (1985)

Whitney   (1987)

I'm Your Baby Tonight   (1990)

The Bodyguard (soundtrack)   (1993)

Waiting to Exhale (soundtrack)   (1995)

The Preacher's Wife (soundtrack)   (1996)

My Love Is Your Love   (1998)

CHRONOLOGY

———— ✿ ————

1963   Whitney Houston born to John and Cissy Houston August 9 in Newark, New Jersey

1968   Begins singing in church at age five

1975   Performs first solo at New Hope Baptist Church in Newark

1977   John and Cissy Houston divorce

1978   Makes professional singing debut with Cissy at Town Hall in New York City

1980   Sings first professional solo; begins modeling

1981   Graduates from Mount St. Dominic Academy in Caldwell, New Jersey; signs a recording contract with agent Eugene Harvey

1982   Records with jazz-funk band Material on the album *One Down*

1983   Records with the Weather Girls; signs with Clive Davis's Arista Records; appears with Davis and Cissy on *The Merv Griffin Show*

1984   Records with Teddy Pendergrass and Jermaine Jackson; works on debut album

1985   *Whitney Houston* released; "You Give Good Love" begins string of number 1 hits

1986   Wins first Grammy Award for best female pop vocal for "Saving All My Love for You"; given key to Newark, New Jersey

1987   *Whitney* enters charts at number 1 after release; Whitney wins second Grammy

1989   Meets Bobby Brown at Soul Train Music Awards; endows Whitney Houston Foundation for Children

1990   Releases *I'm Your Baby Tonight*

1991   Performs national anthem at Super Bowl XXV, creating nationwide sensation; accepts marriage proposal from Brown

1992   Stars in and records the soundtrack to *The Bodyguard*; marries Brown at her mansion on July 18; scores first hit from soundtrack with "I Will Always Love You"

1993   Gives birth to Bobbi Kristina Houston Brown on March 4 in Livingston, New Jersey

1994   Wins three Grammys for *The Bodyguard* soundtrack

1995   Films *Waiting to Exhale*, released at year's end to massive public response; contributes hit song "Exhale (Shoop, Shoop)" to soundtrack

1996   Co-stars in *The Preacher's Wife* with Denzel Washington; records soundtrack, which returns her to her roots in gospel music and yields the hit song "I Believe in You and Me"

1997   Produces and stars in Disney television movie version of the musical "Rodgers and Hammerstein's Cinderella"; the movie garners seven Emmy nominations and wins for Outstanding Art Direction

1998   Releases *My Love Is Your Love*, containing a duet with Mariah Carey, "When You Believe," that is featured in the animated film *The Prince of Egypt*

1999   *My Love Is Your Love* goes platinum

FURTHER READING

Ammons, Kevin, with Nancy Bacon. *Good Girl, Bad Girl: An Insider's Biography of Whitney Houston*. Secaucus, N.J.: Birch Lane Press, 1996.

Bego, Mark. *Whitney!* Toronto/New York: PaperJacks Ltd., 1986.

Christgau, Robert. *Christgau's Record Guide: The '80s.* New York: Pantheon Books, 1990.

DeCurtis, Anthony, and James Henke, with Holly George-Warren. *The Rolling Stone Illustrated History of Rock and Roll.* New York: Random House, 1992.

Hildebrand, Lee. *Stars of Soul and Rhythm & Blues*. New York: Billboard Books, 1994.

INDEX

PICTURE CREDITS

TED COX writes about popular culture and the arts as TV/radio columnist for the *Daily Herald* outside Chicago and as sports columnist for the *Chicago Reader*. He has written about music for both publications and many others. He lives in Chicago with his wife, Catherine, and daughters, Sadie and Megan.

NATHAN IRVIN HUGGINS, one of America's leading scholars in the field of black studies, helped select the titles for the BLACK AMERICANS OF ACHIEVEMENT series, for which he also served as senior consulting editor. He was the W. E. B. Du Bois Professor of History and Afro-American Studies at Harvard University and the director of the W. E. B. Du Bois Institute for Afro-American Research at Harvard. He received his doctorate from Harvard in 1962 and returned there as professor in 1980 after teaching at Columbia University, the University of Massachusetts, Lake Forest College, and the California State University, Long Beach. He was the author of four books and dozens of articles, including *Black Odyssey: The Afro-American Ordeal in Slavery*, *The Harlem Renaissance*, and *Slave and Citizen: The Life of Frederick Douglass*, and was associated with the Children's Television Workshop, National Public Radio, the Boston Athenaeum, the Museum of Afro-American History, the Howard Thurman Educational Trust, and Upward Bound. Professor Huggins died in 1989, at the age of 62, in Cambridge, Massachusetts.